self-talk
for a
calmer
you

Learn how to use positive self-talk
to control anxiety and
live a happier, more relaxed life

BEVERLY D. FLAXINGTON
The Human Behavior Coach

Published by
Adams Media, a division of F+W Media, Inc.
57 Littlefield Street, Avon, MA 02322. U.S.A.
www.adamsmedia.com

ISBN 10: 1-4405-6480-9
ISBN 13: 978-1-4405-6480-2
eISBN 10: 1-4405-6481-7
eISBN13: 978-1-4405-6481-9

Printed in the United States of America.

10   9   8   7   6   5   4   3   2   1

Library of Congress Cataloging-in-Publication Data

Flaxington, Beverly D.
  Self-talk for a calmer you : learn how to use positive self-talk to control anxiety and
live a happier, more relaxed life / Beverly D. Flaxington.
     pages cm
  Includes bibliographical references and index.
  ISBN-13: 978-1-4405-6480-2 (pbk. : alk. paper)
  ISBN-10: 1-4405-6480-9 (pbk. : alk. paper)
  ISBN-13: 978-1-4405-6481-9 (electronic)
  ISBN-10: 1-4405-6481-7 (electronic)
  1. Self-talk. 2. Self-actualization (Psychology) 3. Anxiety. 4. Happiness. I. Title.
BF697.5.S47F585 2013
  613.7'92--dc23   2013018098

Many of the designations used by manufacturers and sellers to distinguish their
product are claimed as trademarks. Where those designations appear in this book and
F+W Media was aware of a trademark claim, the designations have been printed with
initial capital letters.

Cover image © 123rf.com.

This book is available at quantity discounts for bulk purchases.
For information, please call 1-800-289-0963.

Dedication

This book is dedicated to two men who showed me firsthand the power of positive self-talk: Henry Szafarz and Dr. Richard Harte. I will be forever grateful for their precious gift and for the knowledge of how to teach others.

contents

Acknowledgments

With thanks to Peter Archer for his editing talent, to Victoria Sandbrook for finding me and proposing this idea, and to Brendan O'Neill for making it all happen.

Take Charge of Your Anxiety—and Self-Talk

Anxiety is a fact of life for too many people. That's the bad news. The good news is it's fixable.

Everything from getting stuck in traffic to burning the toast to dealing with disappointment in a relationship can fuel the fires of anxiety until our anxious mind can't seem to calm itself down.

This book will show you what anxiety is, how to define it and understand it, and what causes you to become anxious. You will have a chance to complete an assessment to uncover your triggers and causal events. This book is written for anyone who desires a higher quality of emotional life and who is tired of living his or her life in an anxious state.

As you'll see in the following pages, you already have a valuable tool with which to address your anxiety: self-talk. At its most basic level, self-talk is the way you talk to yourself. It's a kind of running internal monologue, a stream of consciousness. As part of the reaction you have to life circumstances, it seems "normal" to have a conversation with yourself about everything you encounter, or might encounter. If you think about that process, you will find that you probably talk to yourself about most things in your life.

This book will show you how to turn that self-talk into an antidote to anxiety. It's a means for you to turn back the waves of panic that sometimes threaten to overwhelm you. How you respond to events in life is infinitely more important than what actually happens to you. You may have heard stories about people overcoming impossible odds to succeed, or about those who rise above their challenges. What they say to themselves, how they interpret the events, what they choose to use as their self-talk is often at the root of their ability to rise and succeed. What makes the difference between those people who seem to overcome the obstacles and make things happen, versus those that get stuck and can't seem to find the way out of their anxious thoughts and feelings? Often it is their self-talk. It's the things people say to themselves to get them through or give them new energy or help them problem solve.

Of course, there's good self-talk and not so good self-talk. In fact, your internal monologue can, sometimes, make things worse. In addition to the actual real-life events—you might, for example, be unable to pay your bills or experience a blow-up fight with your spouse—your anxiety becomes exacerbated by the way you talk to yourself about it: "There is way too much week left over at the end of my money." "My spouse is so rude to me!" "I'm never going to get ahead." These statements and the stories you tell yourself can deepen your anxious responses.

What you should realize, though, is that this negative self-talk is actually within your control. What you will learn from this book is that there is a difference between negative self-talk, which defeats and steals energy, and positive self-talk, which allows you to get up again, shake off the setback, and find a new way.

Everyone knows that anxiety isn't good for your health. Research shows it can raise blood pressure, disrupt sleep, cause digestive problems, and cause an overall feeling of malaise. Some people become so used to living with anxiety that they believe it is the normal state of the mind. They develop a high tolerance for pain and choose to ignore the effects of the anxiety, rather than choosing to take charge of it and manage it differently.

The negative tapes that people play in their subconscious deplete their energy, defeat their best intentions, and leave them by the proverbial side of the road, out of the gas they need to keep going. Replacement scripts with positive self-talk give you a way to calm down. In fact, the scripts you play in your head can affect the outcome of your life circumstances. Knowing what to do and being able to call upon these ideas in any moment is ultimately what makes the difference between those who can manage their self-talk to their advantage and those who are done in by it.

Of course, learning about your self-talk doesn't automatically mean you will have a positive attitude toward everything no matter what happens. Anxiety will still visit you. It can sneak up when you least expect it. But the point is to be prepared for it. What you will learn through this book is how to recognize the visits it makes, what triggers your anxiety, and how to counter it through self-talk. By getting a handle on these things, you can change the game. You will learn how to differentiate between the self-talk that steals and the self-talk that heals. But, the first step to making a positive change is to recognize there is a problem with what you are doing now and to commit that you want this anxious mind to stop causing you pain. Instead you want peace and calm to deal with the challenges of life.

Let's get started on the path to positive, powerful self-talk.

Preparing for the Calmer You

Habits—both good and bad—take a while to develop. Unfortunately you may not have been conscious about which habits are the best ones for you, so some, such as your negative self-talk, may be self-defeating. It will take a concerted effort on your part to turn to positive self-talk on a regular basis to get to the calmer you.

To prepare for your journey, take the following steps:

1. Make a commitment to yourself. Repeat over and over that this matters to you and this is something you want to do. It's a gift you will give yourself, so be sure you are ready to receive it. Positive self-talk will work for you, and it will calm you but only if you are ready to embrace it. If you think it will help, write out your commitment and tape it to your refrigerator, your mirror, or somewhere you'll see it every day to remind you of the journey on which you're embarking.

2. For this project, buy a notebook, purchase an app for your smartphone to keep notes, or set up a Word or Excel

document on your computer. Have something available to record observations, make notes of positive self-talk you want to use, and observe along the way. Don't use the notebook or spreadsheet for anything else. This is all about getting you on the road to positive self-talk.

3. Get a pack of 3" × 5" cards. You'll often be asked to write things down, so keep the cards in a handy, visible place.

4. Find or create a safe and comfortable place you are able to go to do some of the exercises. This could be a space within a room in your house, or it could be somewhere else; it doesn't matter as long as you feel comfortable and relaxed there. It needs to be somewhere you won't be interrupted by phone calls, family, or any other distractions. It needn't be large—just a place to sit and focus.

5. Be sure to keep this book handy at all times. This journey will involve many aspects of your life, your work, your relationships, and your day-to-day activities. You want to have the information ready at your fingertips when you need it.

Spending a few minutes preparing will give you the tools you need at the ready as you begin this odyssey to the calmer you. Let's start now.

part I

CHAPTER 1

Anxiety and the Importance of Self-Talk

Anxiety. Even the word itself might make you feel anxious. If the statistics are accurate, 20–30 percent of the population suffers from some form of anxiety at some point in our adult lives. At any point in time, that's almost 20 million people walking around feeling ill at ease. While some level of anxiety about life circumstances is normal, for some people it becomes debilitating and can turn into full-blown fear or disorders. For such people, the quality of life suffers because anxiety disrupts their everyday enjoyment of life, the ability to be content, or even their potential for success. There are two types of anxiety: the everyday feeling of worry or uneasiness, and phobias or other similar conditions. In this chapter, we'll talk about both of these types.

Where's It Coming From?

The biggest problem with resolving anxiety is that often it is hard to identify a cause or even why you feel anxious. You can't pinpoint it. It's just a feeling that things aren't right and you don't feel happy or content. Various negative life experiences convince many people the world isn't a safe place. These can be traumatic events in their childhood, disappointments they have encountered, or other troubles they have seen. Even though those events are in the past, they can produce ongoing anxious feelings in the present. In fact, some people use anxiety as a coping mechanism to protect themselves from negative experiences. To be confident and feel good leads to failure, so better to feel anxious and uptight and be prepared!

Almost everyone has some bad experiences, trauma, or letdowns in their lives. Those who have more than their fair share may conclude that life just isn't a safe place. They live with a consistent sense of disappointment.

Before we take up the cure for this anxiety, let's understand a bit more about what it is. We can also help you identify what type of anxiety you suffer from.

The "Blahs"

Many people suffer from an everyday form of anxiety commonly referred to as "the blahs." This can be hard to recognize because often it isn't connected to a specific event or situation. Instead it is just there.

Anxiety and Fear

People sometimes equate anxiety with fear, but they're actually different. Fear is a response to negative stimuli: a dangerous situation you are about to face, or the worry you are not going to pass an upcoming important test. There is something in particular you feel fearful about. Fear is useful, since it motivates you to action—if you see an oncoming car bearing down on you, fear impels you to jump out of the way.

Everyday anxiety is that free-floating feeling that something is wrong. You can't really put your finger on it, but the world, your life, or your feelings just don't seem right. *What's wrong with me?* you think. *Why is everyone else happy and I feel so blah?* You may feel as if "something bad is going to happen" or that there is something you should be worrying about without knowing exactly what it is. You're waiting for the other shoe to drop when the first one hasn't even dropped yet!

If you suffer from everyday anxiety you may rarely experience joy. Life just doesn't seem fun because there is something always nagging at the back of your mind. Even when things are not overtly bad, there is a lingering sense that the world just isn't right. Everyday anxiety can steal your mental health, your emotional confidence, and your physical well-being. It can cause sleeplessness, lack of appetite, overeating, low-grade depression, and a variety of physical ailments such as upset stomach, headaches, or nervous tics.

A Common Experience

Many people suffer anxiety in silence. They are embarrassed to admit how afraid they feel, or how much they worry. The experience of anxiety is more common than we may think. According to the National Institute of Mental Health (NIMH), approximately 40 million American adults aged eighteen and older, or about 18.1 percent of people in this age group, in a given year, have an anxiety disorder.

Diagnosed Anxiety Disorders

In addition to everyday anxiety, there are a number of diagnosed anxiety disorders. These disorders are a more serious form of anxiety that often require medical treatment.

The six most commonly diagnosed anxiety disorders are:

- **Panic Disorder.** Characterized by a sudden, unreasoning feeling of terror, often accompanied by chest pains, tightening or constricting of the throat, palpitations, and profuse sweating. Although the terror is real, as are the physical consequences, the event is not.

- **Obsessive-Compulsive Disorder (OCD).** People with OCD engage in compulsive rituals, fearful something terrible will happen if they do not. They obsess over something and develop compulsive behavior in an effort to "cure" the obsession.

- **Posttraumatic Stress Disorder (PTSD).** It is most commonly associated with military personnel returning from war but applies to anyone who has anxiety resulting from a terrifying real event.

- **Social Anxiety Disorder.** This disorder afflicts people who are anxious in the presence of a lot of people. This can include everything from going to the supermarket or the train station to being at a party with friends or in a work environment.

- **Phobias.** These are fears and anxious feelings, resulting from particular things or situations. Even a reminder of the object of fear can cause anxiety: Someone with a fear of flying, for example, may not be able to look at a picture of an airplane.

- **Generalized Anxiety Disorder.** This is nonspecific anxiety that becomes so exaggerated and so pervasive that excessive worry, tension, fear, and dread are the norm. Physical symptoms can include headaches, backaches, nausea, irritable bowel syndrome, and temporomandibular joint disorder (jaw pain that often comes about from excessive gritting or grinding of teeth).

Stopping the Anxious Cycle

Anxiety is not a condition to be "cured," but it can be recognized, managed, and dealt with more effectively. The first step, as in any behavioral change, is recognizing that anxiety visits you and how it appears. Only then can you begin to head it off and turn your attention to more positive, productive ideas.

Seeing Anxiety in Action

In order to understand how anxiety affects you and find a path to overcoming it, it's important to see it in action. Just as you wouldn't allow a friend who constantly upsets you to stay with you indefinitely, you must find a way to keep anxiety at a distance.

The problem is that anxiety is stealthy. We don't say to ourselves, "How anxious can I get today? I'm hoping to break my all-time anxious record and have this be my most difficult day yet!" People who deal with anxiety find it looming in the background (and sometimes the forefront) of their daily life.

Some people accept it as a fact of life. They believe everyone worries all the time.

Emotionally, you'll find that anxiety leads to depression or outbursts of anger. It can make you unable to concentrate or to do simple tasks well, or it can cloud your view so that you don't see things clearly. Physically, it will give you symptoms ranging from stomachaches and headaches to acid reflux.

By the same token, though, once you start to turn your self-talk around and push anxiety away, you'll find that these symptoms disappear. You'll be mentally, emotionally, and physically healthier, and the change will be obvious to those with whom you interact. Insofar as many real illnesses arise because of anxiety and its partner, stress, dealing with anxiety will make you less subject to maladies.

Locating the Source of Your Anxiety

How can you start to turn things around? The first step is to recognize that you're anxious. The second step is to pinpoint the site of that anxiety. For each person it's different, but there are some general places from which anxiety can derive, and some common things can set it into motion.

- Fears often develop as a result of some real-life or imagined experience. Fears unchecked can turn into phobias, which can be very debilitating. While fear arises in reaction to something—for example, you are afraid of failing an important test you need to pass to keep your job—phobias can prevent you from even confronting the source of your fear. If you have a phobia about taking tests, you probably can't even walk into the test room. The first positive step here is to *recognize the source of your fear*.

- Stress is often a normal reaction to the everyday experiences of life. The world throws out difficult things to deal with on a regular basis. Stress, like fear, has its place. It can be a catalyst to spur you on. It can give you the energy and ideas you need to cope effectively with life circumstances. Here positive self-talk plays an essential role in turning bad stress into creative stress. You must *recognize whether the stress you feel is empowering or enfeebling you.*

- Your past life experiences can contribute to anxious states. You might have grown up in an unsafe environment or have experienced trauma at a young age. The past can lead to difficulty primarily if you let it dominate your present. Here, too, your self-talk must begin by *understanding what part of your past is causing anxiety in the present.*

Negative Self-Talk

Anxiety can be the result of actual events (for example, you're anxious because you're behind on your bills), or it can be because of faulty thinking (you tell yourself you're irresponsible and will inevitably get behind with your bills, even if you haven't up to this point). Negative self-talk works on both types of anxiety, but it's most pernicious in the second kind: A person has experienced an event or anticipates an event and talks negatively to herself about the event. The result: the event becomes worse. Self-talk—the things you say to yourself and the "tapes" of conversations or thoughts you play in your head—is often the difference between whether anxiety will diminish or will continue to grow in difficulty.

In the next chapter, we'll consider self-talk in more detail and discover how it can go from being an enemy to becoming a valued friend.

CHAPTER 2

Self-Talk and You

When you walked out your front door this morning, you engaged in self-talk. Mentally, probably without even thinking about it, you asked yourself some questions:

- "Do I have my keys?"
- "Which corner does the bus stop on, was it this one or that one?"
- "How much money do I need for the bus and for lunch today?"

Along with these questions, you probably asked some that are concerned with longer-range issues, such as, "Do I have enough money in my savings account to take that trip to Florida?" You probably also reminded yourself of what you need to do today and made some random observations about your life and the people in it:

- "I need to get that insurance form in by Friday. I will put it somewhere so I remember to send it on time."
- "I can't go into that job interview now. I have a bad cold and I won't be confident."
- "My parents are such jerks—everyone else can go out late on Friday night except me. I hate my life."

The constant voice chatters away to you all day long, giving you the play-by-play on your life.

The Enemy: Negative Self-Talk

The real problem comes when your self-talk steals opportunities from you or pushes you toward actions that aren't good for you. This is when you find yourself engaging in self-defeating behavior such as lashing out at someone in anger, or just upset, depressed, and lacking confidence. The self-talk wears you down and tells you how bad things are. After listening to it over and over again, you start to believe it. Self-talk can become so familiar to you that you don't even notice its existence. You may not think of it as talking to yourself, you may just think of it as noting what's going on around you. While negative self-talk is a constant visitor for many, it's not your friend. It isn't helping you in any way.

That's the bad news. The good news is you can change your self-talk. It's not set in stone and immutable. Self-talk—*positive* self-talk—can be a valued ally in the fight against anxiety. To turn negative into positive, though, you have to listen to what you say to yourself when things aren't going well. What thoughts do you have when you encounter a difficult situation? Begin to bring the self-talk into the light so you can see it and work with it more effectively.

For example, maybe you are struggling in your job. Your negative self-talk script runs something like, "I will never be able to please this boss. No matter how hard I work, he doesn't appreciate me." Or perhaps it is personal relationships where you encounter negativity. "How did I ever decide to marry this person?" you say to yourself. "I can't stand her. She isn't even my type. I hate sitting down at the dinner table every night with her. Why didn't I marry my high school sweetheart instead? We would be so happy now."

This is the way that negative self-talk takes over. But imagine what it would be like if you turned this around. If you said to yourself, "Wow! I'm so lucky I'm married to a wonderful spouse! I value our time together. It's true that we have some differences, but we can work on them, and compared to the benefits I get from this marriage emotionally and in every other way, that's a small price to pay." You'd feel a surge of good feeling every time you saw your spouse. It would be enjoyable to spend time in her or his company. That's what can happen when positive self-talk takes over.

Reading some of these negative lines, you might be wondering how I know what's going on in your life and in your mind. The truth is that I'm not clairvoyant—negative self-talk isn't that creative! Different people in similar situations often talk to themselves in the same way.

Negative self-talk can even occur when things are going right for you. It plays with insidious skill on your fear of failure: "It's too good right now. I'm due for something bad to happen."

How Important Is Your Self-Talk?

What you say to yourself, the words you play in your head, is often the difference between a healthy and an unhealthy life. Think of negative self-talk as something that helps anxiety fuel the emotional flames, while positive self-talk is a bucket of water you can throw on it to douse the fire. The key lies in identifying your habits in relationship to your self-talk, recognizing what your self-talk says to you and why, and understanding its impact. When you recognize these components, you will get a clearer understanding of how self-talk can help you.

Because you have probably lived with it for so long, and in so many different venues, you may not realize when it sneaks up and begins talking to you. In most cases, it is only after you notice that you feel badly, are angry, or are depressed that you even notice the voices are telling you negative things.

Who Is That Talking to You?

The voices telling you what's real, how to think, and what to do next come from many places. You might recognize words you learned from your mother, father, or an older sibling. You might hear the voice of a reporter on the news, a teacher from your past, or a difficult boss. Many times the voices are an amalgam of people you have heard from throughout your life.

CASE STUDY

Let's look at an example of negative self-talk that comes from the past but has a powerful impact on the present.

Andrew is a successful entrepreneur, managing a small consulting business that employs ten people and is rapidly growing. He works hard and tries to make time for his family, but somehow work always seems to come first. Even on the weekends and on family vacations, he's never far away from his cell phone and his laptop. This has already put a strain on his family life, but matters came to a head recently when he missed his daughter's dance recital because he felt he had to work late at the office. He came home to an angry spouse and a child in tears.

Andrew knows he's got a problem with working too much. He's even tried to do something about it, delegating more work to his employees and even, at one point, consulting a therapist. But now it's getting very serious and threatening his family.

What Andrew may not know is that his difficulty is rooted in self-talk, which in turn has its origins in his childhood. His father, who struggled to make ends meet when Andrew was growing up, was a stern taskmaster. He berated Andrew frequently for being "lazy," "a slacker," and for "lying about and expecting the world to give you a living."

The result is that always in Andrew's mind there's the voice of his father, hectoring him, pushing him to work more, and telling him that if he doesn't, he'll be a failure. Success only comes from hard work. Nobody owes you anything. You've got to struggle for everything you get, and nothing comes before that.

Of course, there's some truth behind these sentiments, but this self-talk has pushed Andrew's life seriously out of balance. Even when he's driving home from work in the evening, his negative self-talk is whispering to him that he shouldn't have left the office with tasks yet undone. The result is that although he knows intellectually that he should make more time for his family, emotionally he's still tied to his father's voice.

Fortunately for Andrew, his therapist knows the power of self-talk, both negative and positive. She leads Andrew through a discussion of his childhood, allowing him to express his feelings about his father and come to terms with them. She explains to him the importance of finding positive self-talk along these lines: "I am *not* my father. I'm me. I'm successful and I have good employees who will do their jobs and help ensure the success of my business. The whole point of making money and achieving financial security is to allow me to spend time with the people I love. So when I go home at night, I'm not running away from work; I'm going back to my family—the most important part of my life."

By repeating these words to himself, Andrew is able, gradually, to quiet his father's voice and find a better, healthier work-life balance.

What Do You Say When . . .

In this chapter you will identify the primary areas of your negative self-talk. You may find that they change over time—your job may be going well right now but personal relationships are more of an issue for you. Or you've just been fired from your job, but your family is supportive.

If I asked you if you like talking to yourself about things that make you feel badly, most likely you would answer, "No." That's understandable: Most people don't enjoy being scolded or talked down to, and few people thrive in environments where they are consistently reminded of how terrible things are! You probably don't want to experience the negativity that consumes your mind, but—and this is a very important point—you may not realize it's there. It may be so familiar that it feels necessary and welcome.

We mentioned earlier that self-talk is stealthy. One minute you're feeling optimistic and excited about your day, and the next you're filled with dread and anxiety about what you are going to face. Or one minute you may be a bit depressed, and the next minute you find yourself yelling at your child or screaming obscenities at the driver who edged in front of you in traffic. The transition is so sneaky that you don't realize you've let negative self-talk take over.

That's where the assessments in this chapter come in.

Assessing Your Negative Self-Talk

Right now you might be saying, "I'm anxious, but I don't talk to myself about it. That's what crazy people do." Most people don't walk around thinking about the voices in their head. And yet, we know they are there. The first important step on the road we'll take together is uncovering the source of your negative self-talk. You want to see where it comes from and learn what those voices say to you. This exercise will help you locate some sources of your negative self-talk and see how they visit you.

Complete this section when you have some time to sit quietly and answer the questions. You will need time to think, and then you will need to be aware of what you are doing each day, in order to capture enough information to work with as you complete this book.

Review the following list of twenty life experiences. Rate how anxious each of the following makes you, *in general*. Use a scale of 1–10. 1 represents "Not at all anxious about this"; 10 represents "Extremely anxious and agitated about this."

Everyday events, such as getting stuck in traffic or burning the toast	1 2 3 4 5 6 7 8 9 10
My work situation	1 2 3 4 5 6 7 8 9 10
My boss	1 2 3 4 5 6 7 8 9 10
My family of origin (mom, dad, siblings, stepfamily)	1 2 3 4 5 6 7 8 9 10
My spouse or significant other	1 2 3 4 5 6 7 8 9 10
My child or children	1 2 3 4 5 6 7 8 9 10
My home life	1 2 3 4 5 6 7 8 9 10
My current level of mental health	1 2 3 4 5 6 7 8 9 10
My current level of physical health	1 2 3 4 5 6 7 8 9 10
Thinking about my health in the future	1 2 3 4 5 6 7 8 9 10
My financial situation	1 2 3 4 5 6 7 8 9 10
My living situation	1 2 3 4 5 6 7 8 9 10
Caring for others in my life	1 2 3 4 5 6 7 8 9 10
The list of things I have to do	1 2 3 4 5 6 7 8 9 10

Commitments I have made, or someone will expect me to make	1	2	3	4	5	6	7	8	9	10
External events such as the economy	1	2	3	4	5	6	7	8	9	10
External events such as environmental or social conditions	1	2	3	4	5	6	7	8	9	10
What might happen tomorrow	1	2	3	4	5	6	7	8	9	10
Thinking about my personal future	1	2	3	4	5	6	7	8	9	10
What happened already—today, yesterday, or in the past	1	2	3	4	5	6	7	8	9	10
Regrets about my past, or things I have done	1	2	3	4	5	6	7	8	9	10
Guilt over how I live my life now	1	2	3	4	5	6	7	8	9	10
My feelings of "self" and self-worth	1	2	3	4	5	6	7	8	9	10

Now review the list. Circle those things for which you chose a 6 or greater to describe your anxious reaction.

On the worksheet below, identify the first thing that comes to mind when you read the line. For example, if you chose an 8 on "Commitments I have made, or someone will expect me to make," you might write, "Too many people want something from me. I have no time to do everything I'm expected to do." Or, if you chose "My family of origin" as a 9 or 10 on the scale, you might write, "Anyone who grew up with two alcoholic parents would check a 9 or 10 on this scale. Isn't it obvious how anxiety-inducing that has been for me?"

Your mind tells you something related to the subject that you circled. When you circled a number higher than 5, you thought, "Yes, this is anxiety-inducing for me." What you write about what you think, feel, or say to yourself about this subject is important.

Number _____ What I say to myself about it:

_____

_____

_____

Number _____ What I say to myself about it:

_____

_____

_____

Number _____ What I say to myself about it:

_____

_____

_____

Number _____ What I say to myself about it:

_____

_____

_____

Number _____ What I say to myself about it:

_____

_____

_____

Number _____ What I say to myself about it:

_____

_____

_____

Number _____ What I say to myself about it:

_____

_____

_____

Now go back and reread what you have written. These subjects, and what you say to yourself about them, will give you some clues about how negative self-talk creeps into your thought patterns.

Card Assessment

As an additional exercise, write the subjects from the list of twenty items in the exercise above on separate 3" × 5" index cards or a small sheet of paper you can keep nearby as you go through your day. You might have an index card that says "My family of origin" at the top of it. As you encounter situations or thoughts about the subject, write down the negative self-talk you find yourself using. Be as specific as you can. If you do this on a regular basis, say for two or three weeks, you should have a filled index card that has a number of negative statements you make to yourself about the subject. If you fill one card or sheet of paper, take another one. Keep adding to it until you can get a clearer and clearer view of exactly what you say in reaction to the subject or situation. Remember that awareness is an important first step. Before you can implement new ideas to use positive self-talk, you must be aware of the sneaky negative self-talk that comes in and steals from you.

Keep these cards nearby as you continue with exercises in the book. Knowing exactly how you react and the negative self-talk you use allows you to become better at recognizing it and dealing with it more positively and effectively.

Anxiety and Its Impact

Now that we have some idea of your major sources of anxiety, it's time to look at how you react to them and at the resulting negative self-talk's impact on you. Learning how negative self-talk impacts you is like having an early warning system. If you know a tornado is coming, you will seek cover or go somewhere safe. Similarly, you want to turn on your positive self-talk to protect you and keep you confident.

This next section will require you to take time to observe your reactions and actions with regard to stressful situations. It's important for you to recognize how events unfold for you. You can always learn from talking to others about their anxieties, but in order to make change happen, you must know your own impacts.

Get Specific

It's possible that you aren't currently experiencing anxiety and feel things are "okay." While I recommend you continue reading, you should keep the book handy and pick it up when you are anxious about something so you can record the data. You'll learn lots of things from this book, but the most useful ones will be the most specific to you. Most people don't take charge of their lives because they aren't exactly sure what to do. By the time anxiety has taken over, their mind is fraught with worry and negative self-talk—a runaway train that no one can stop. You want to pull the levers to stop that train long before it gets to a final crash.

Think about how anxiety impacts you. For example, if you say you get headaches when you're stressed, do they make it hard for you to function through your day? Is the effect cumulative? You miss work because the headaches are bad but then the lost sick day creates more stress and more headaches.

In this assessment you're going to identify how the negative self-talk, or anxious reaction to conditions in your life, manifests. Learning about impact helps to identify what are commonly called triggers, which we'll discuss later in this chapter.

Anxiety has a direct impact on you. It can be emotional (worry, faulty thinking, lack of confidence, lack of enjoyment of life) or physical (stomachache, sweaty palms, or stressed muscles and headaches). Whatever the symptoms, there is *some* impact. It's important to understand how anxiety impacts you so that you can use your mind and body to alert you to its onset. Once you learn to decode anxiety's effect on you, you can often go back and locate its source. Once you locate the source, you can change your self-talk.

Review the list of those things that you consider to be most anxiety-inducing for you. How do you react in these situations? Do they make you feel depressed? Do you yell at someone? Do you grit your teeth and fume? Do you feel unable to get out of bed in the morning when you have to deal with the situation? Do you get an upset stomach?

On the worksheet below, list the situation. "My family of origin" might be one. Next to it, identify any impact you are aware of that anxiety about this subject has on you. You might say to yourself, "They just make me crazy!" But what do you do as a result? Do you bang a fist against the wall? Yell? Do you repress your emotions and as a result feel sick to your stomach? Do you get clammy hands or a nervous tic? Identify what happens here:

Situation: _____

Impact: _____

_____

Situation: _____

Impact: _____

_____

Situation: _____

Impact: _____

_____

Situation: _____

Impact: _____

_____

Situation: _____

Impact: _____

_____

Situation: _____

Impact: _____

_____

Start with the Impact

Are you not exactly sure how the impact relates to the situation? If this is the case, go at the exercise a bit differently. Start by identifying your negative responses and then try to connect them back to anxious situations.

First, identify a negative feeling you have—mental, physical, or emotional: _____

_____

Next, identify when you experience this negative feeling. Is it all of the time? Is it in reaction to something? Is it in the morning as you think about your day? Is it when your mother calls? Identify any associations you can make with it:

_____

_____

_____

Repeat this exercise with as many physical, emotional, and mental symptoms as you can identify.

Back to the Cards

If you are having a hard time connecting anything clearly enough to write it now, that's okay. Take the 3" × 5" cards you used in the previous exercise and make notes of the impact you experience in the situation. Don't just write the negative self-talk; include any and all sensations or experiences related to the anxious situation. So, for example, if you find yourself getting uptight in traffic (an everyday event you might have noted as anxiety arousing), write the negative self-talk but also capture how you physically or mentally react. Do you grip the steering wheel tightly? Do you feel a pounding behind your temples? Does your stomach churn and burn? Don't write while you are driving, of course, but make a mental note and capture these symptoms when you can.

What Situations Stress You?

Another way to identify impact is to examine situations that bother you or where you have had a negative reaction in the past. Review this next list and see if any of these common situations resonate with you. Write some ideas down here, too. The more data you can gather, the more you will see themes or common ideas that are anxiety-inducing for you.

1. My biggest area of disappointment in life is _____

   _____

   _____

2. The thing that frustrates me the most is _____

   _____

   _____

3. I really hate it when _____

   _____

   _____

4. I get so stressed out when _____

   _____

   _____

5. Things that "bug me" include_____

   _____

   _____

6. I get irritated by_____

   _____

   _____

7. I would be happy in life if only I didn't _____

   _____

   _____

8. People really annoy me when they _____

   _____

   _____

9. It's not fair that I _____

   _____

   _____

Review this list and check it against the list on which you circled things that were the most anxiety arousing for you. Are there themes? Are there areas you specifically want to target now? Write any thoughts you have now here: _____

_____

_____

_____

Objectivity Is Important!

When you start to understand your responses and reactions, don't take it as an opportunity to beat up on yourself or engage in negative self-talk. Instead, approach this as a scientist. When you are first trying to learn and assess, you're not making judgments; you are simply gathering data. You will understand how to use this information later. For now, seek the facts. Understand the situations and the impact. Be willing to learn.

The Little Engine of Self-Talk

As made clear earlier, while negative self-talk is highly destructive, positive self-talk is the solution to your anxiety. It spurs you on. It reminds you of the strengths you have, and it can build your confidence to do what you need to do.

Think of the famous story about the Little Engine That Could. "I think I can, I think I can, I think I can," the engine puffs to itself. It self-talks its way to the top of a mountain, hauling a long train full of circus animals. Self-talk is a good friend, reminding you of your strengths and your past successes. When you use self-talk in a positive way, it gives you a much-needed boost.

Changing from negative to positive self-talk doesn't alter any facts about your situation. What it changes is your attitude, giving you more power to deal with things. Having a positive mental attitude and believing in yourself and your ability to overcome obstacles will often make the difference in whether you can achieve your goal or not. Many studies show that when you're ill, a positive mindset can lead to a remission of the disease. At a minimum, engaging in positive self-talk will help you frame the situation in your life a bit more positively. The events you're confronting are just that—objective situations. It's the interpretation, or the lens through which those events are filtered, that's causing you distress.

Talking a Different Talk

The key to changing your self-talk from negative to positive is recognizing where your self-talk starts and what it says to you. From there you can understand the impact of your self-talk. Without this, you can't make choices about how to handle it. In this chapter, you've taken a large step toward doing this by completing the assessments and evaluating what sort of situations trigger your self-talk.

In the next chapter, you will locate the sources of your self-talk and complete an assessment to further clarify your triggers and reactions. But first let's look at how self-talk becomes your "truth."

An Everyday Event: How Self-Talk Unfolds

Most people don't enjoy being scolded or talked down to, and few people thrive in environments where they are consistently reminded of how terrible things are. You probably don't want to experience negativity. The problem is that unbeknownst to you and unplanned, your mind starts to niggle at something and you become agitated and upset. Possibly someone says something irritating, triggering a reaction. The transition is so sneaky that you don't realize you have moved from positive self-talk to negative self-talk. Let's look at a short example of this.

Is a Note Just a Note?

Imagine it is a Wednesday and you're getting ready to go to work. You feel energized; you have had a good night's sleep; and you have time to stop for a nice cup of coffee. As you are putting your coat on the hook and booting your computer, you notice that your boss has left a note on your desk saying she wants to talk with you as soon as you have a chance.

Let's look at this objectively: It is a note on your desk, written by your boss, asking for a chance to talk. There is nothing good, or bad, about the situation. It's simply a note on the desk.

However, your self-talk kicks in and interprets the situation. A note is no longer just a note. If you have had a negative encounter with your boss or you generally believe that the workplace is not friendly, the note is a "warning" from your boss or a "summons" to her office. Your anxiety level starts to rise. Viewing the note through the lens of your past experiences, you might say to yourself, "Oh no—I hate when she leaves notes like this. It's always an omen that there is some new project she wants me to take on that I don't want to do. I haven't even finished the project I am working on now—what a slave driver she is."

Of course, at this stage you have not even responded to the boss's note, and yet you have had a whole experience with it. Think about that. *Nothing has happened!* You walked in and saw the note. But internally you've told yourself a whole story about the meaning of the note. The practical upshot is that when you walk into the boss's office, you'll probably have some attitude. After all, you "know" what the boss will say to you, so you act on it before you even have the conversation.

Of course the opposite could happen, too. If your experiences with your boss have generally been positive, you'll see the note and think: "She is such a sweetheart. I know she wants to recognize me for my current project. I have been working so hard on this and am feeling so good about crossing the finish line and getting it done. She probably wants to give me her kudos and congratulate me on a job well done. She is the best boss I have ever had. I am going to get over to her office right away and see what's going on."

Your positive self-talk might put you in a confident mood. You are eager to speak to her and walk into her office ready for her accolades. Your attitude tells you, "This was just a sign of how right I was that this was going to be a good day. I *knew* I felt good when I woke up this morning!"

The Viewer as Interpreter

Now, stop for a minute and consider both of these situations. The objective situation is still there—you walked into the office and took your coat off. Then you read a note. How did this become a play with characters and action and expectations? What happened, of course, is that you started talking to yourself about the note. You made up a story about it and extended this story to include your work environment. Whether the story was good or bad probably depended heavily on past experiences with your boss or your attitude toward bosses in general.

This scenario can help you understand how two people can experience the same event and have differing self-talk about it. Imagine a colleague happens to walk into your cubicle or office right after you picked up the note. Your self-talk has already kicked in, for better or worse. A story line is unfolding in your mind about what will happen once you go see the boss.

But now, with another interpreter on the scene, things can change. Perhaps your colleague notices the note and has a very different reaction. Though you think the boss is an ogre, your coworker finds her to be a wonderful, supportive human being. You are stewing about the note and what you will encounter once you walk through the boss's doorway. Your colleague is telling you, "What do you mean it's a bad omen? I love when she leaves me notes like this one; it usually means she wants to thank me for my efforts!"

Two people see something as innocuous as a note and have dramatically different reactions. It happens all the time. We each interpret a situation with our relevant self-talk, which is unique to us. If interpretation were not at the root of how we translate and understand a situation, then we would all see things the same way. The facts would be the facts.

Self-Talk Tells You What's Real—But Is It?

Self-talk is what you tell yourself to interpret the conditions you experience. But sometimes it can seem as if self-talk itself *is* the experience. People take facts, data, and information and interpret them. The problem is that negative self-talk emphasizes things that can deepen your anxiety. Positive self-talk, on the other hand, helps ground you in reality. Learning to be more objective is important to managing self-talk.

CHAPTER 3

Finding Your Triggers

Have you ever been convinced of something without evidence? You "just knew" that your friend wanted something from you. You "just knew" that the boss had it in for you. You "just knew" the checkout person at the grocery store disliked your face. Then, when you had the chance to learn more about the situation, you learned you could not have been more wrong. All human beings sometimes "feel things in our bones." What is the reason we feel that way?

What Pulls Your Trigger?

What you're seeing at work are what therapists call "triggers." Triggers are those things that set you off. They are the catalyst that kicks your negative self-talk into gear. In order to disarm them, you must first learn what they are.

Think of your trigger as a match. For the match to light, you must scratch it on a surface or hold it to a flame. If you hold the match up and do nothing else, nothing will happen. In the same way, your negative self-talk is triggered when you're scratched against something. Somehow your mind comes in contact with an event or condition that causes it distress. This triggers something inside of you—like the match striking the right surface—that ignites your negative self-talk. But just as you can blow out the match, so you can extinguish your negative self-talk once you realize it's there.

Triggers can be anything from words people use that "irritate" you to someone's tone of voice to something you see that you don't like. They set the negative self-talk cycle in motion.

Thirteen Triggers

Let's look at a short list of thirteen life circumstances that can be tremendously anxiety-inducing in most people. If these circumstances are among your triggers (and there's a good chance that at least one of them is), the resulting negative self-talk limits your ability to think clearly, to be creative, and to problem solve. You may become stumped about how to get through the situation or deal with it more effectively. Review this list and see whether you connect to anything herein. As you read each one, stop for a moment and think about it. Does this situation resonate with you? Do you have a negative, anxiety-based reaction to it? If so, consider using a journal to track when you experience this situation and how it triggers you. Capture the self-talk you currently use as you react to it. Remember, awareness is the first step—once you are aware, you can make choices to respond differently next time.

1. Job stress due to people—an unhappy boss, for example, or coworkers who don't respond to you in a timely fashion
2. Job stress due to the work itself—such as the problem of too much to do and not enough time to do it
3. Problems with people—a spouse with an addiction, for instance, or a combative family member
4. Poor communication with those you care about
5. Unmet goals or dreams in your life
6. Disruptions—financial woes, sickness, loss of a spouse, having to move to a new location
7. Physical pain related to ongoing medical conditions or a general feeling of malaise
8. Discovery that a spouse or significant other has been unfaithful or has lied to you
9. Broken relationships with parents or children
10. Worries about the future—college funding, for example, or retirement or being alone
11. General fears such as public speaking, flying, or social anxiety
12. Dislike of government, whether officials or policies
13. Worries about the world in general

CASE STUDY

Let's see how this business of triggers works in practice.

Alice has just started work at a new job in a bank. She left her previous job as administrative assistant because her boss was verbally abusive. Every minor error she made was used as an excuse to jerk her onto the managerial carpet for a reprimand. The boss made cold, cutting remarks to her about her ability and seemed to enjoy making her feel small. Alice came home every night and collapsed on the sofa in tears. Often her sleep was interrupted as she tossed and turned worrying about the next day.

Alice was relieved to leave the toxic environment and was pleased when she was offered a job at the bank. In addition, it made for an easier commute than her previous position, and she was told that it was possible to move up to other positions within the bank. Best of all, her boss seemed kind and considerate.

The fourth day on the job, Alice got a short e-mail from her boss, pointing out a small error in one of her memos and asking her to redo it. Before she could even think about the request from her boss, she sat at her desk, trembling, and then had to go into the restroom for ten minutes to calm down. She found that her hands were shaking so badly that she had trouble adjusting her makeup.

What happened? After all, it was a very minor matter—the sort of thing that happens millions of times to millions of people. Yet to Alice, initially, it was an epic disaster.

The answer is that her boss's note hit one of Alice's triggers. Because of her experience with her previous employer, she was highly sensitive to having her work criticized. Her negative self-talk kicked in immediately: "See? You can't do anything right. You're incompetent at your job—you can't even write a simple memo without messing up. You'll probably be out the door in a week. The boss will see you can't hack it."

Fortunately, Alice had taken the time and trouble to think about the way in which her previous job had affected her. She recognized that the note had set off one of her triggers and that her emotional response to it was both irrational and potentially self-destructive. So, with an effort, she turned her self-talk around.

"I can fix this problem. After all, I'm good at my job. This just means I have to be extra-careful with the work I submit to my boss. But I'm confident I can do that and win her trust. I am happy she is a clear communicator and tells me what she needs and how she needs it done. This will help me to be more successful."

Alice followed up on her positive self-talk, making sure she proofread all her memos twice and took her time to ensure they were carefully prepared. Her boss noticed and complimented her on her attention to detail. And within six months, Alice moved up to a higher position within the company.

Word Associations and Assessment

To further understand the source of your triggers that ignite the negative self-talk, let's play some word association. Below is a list of phrases. Read each phrase and think about it. Next to it, write a word that comes to mind when you hear this phrase. Your word should describe an emotion or a response set off by the word. So, for example, next to the phrase "The color blue" you might place the word "peaceful." On the other hand, if you hate blue, you might write "unpleasant" or "ugly."

Don't overthink this process. There are no right or wrong answers. This exercise is simply to allow your mind to associate ideas with each of these areas and let them come to the surface so you can work with them more effectively. Be sure to keep your response to only one or two words. Think in terms of rapid response answers. This isn't a writing project; it's a way to get your gut, initial reaction on paper to different scenarios in your life. Ready? Begin!

Job-Related Words

My boss_____

My job_____

My employer_____

Going on an interview_____

Public speaking _____

My workplace_____

Communication at my workplace _____

Job satisfaction or fulfillment _____

Personal Relationships

My parents_____

My siblings _____

My children_____

My spouse or significant other_____

My grandchildren _____

My extended family _____

My friends _____

My social life_____

Life Circumstances and Life Change

My current state in life _____

Achieving my goals _____

My level of happiness_____

My health_____

The health of my family _____

Stressors, Worries, and Fears

My ability to manage stress _____

Time management _____

Taking care of myself_____

My relationship with food _____

Now take a moment to look at what you have written on the lines next to these words and common scenarios. Take a red pen and circle those words you wrote that are negative or give you a negative feeing or thought. So if you wrote "Good guy" or "Fair" for your boss, don't circle anything. However, if you wrote "Suffocating" or "Difficult," put a red circle around the entire line from "My boss" to "Difficult" or "Suffocating." Go back through the list and take the time to identify those words that are anxiety-inducing, negative, or might create a feeling of fear or worry in you.

Capturing Your Negativity Themes

As you look over the list of circled negative words, do you find any themes? Of course, it's possible you have negative words written next to everything. People who are diagnosed with anxiety, or who live with a general sense that something is wrong all of the time, will find their reactions to most life conditions being a negative response. But mostly you'll find there are themes on the list. Perhaps all of your negative comments concerned the relationships in your life. Possibly they were about health. See if you can group the responses into themes. Use the lines below here to do this:

My Negativity Themes:

_____

_____

_____

Keep these themes in mind as you continue the assessment process. If you have identified specific areas, focus your attention on the following chapters that most closely fit your concerns. If you have a general feeling of "Life stinks and makes me anxious all the time," you will find that going through each chapter and learning techniques for incorporating positive self-talk is important.

Assessing Trigger Responses

When the trigger happens, a response follows it. It's important to recognize how your triggers affect you. Sometimes it helps to mentally go to the event or circumstance that triggered you—starting from the point you felt the symptoms of anxiety.

The Unseen Cycle

You experience something in life—large or small. Rather than see it as what it is—an objective experience—you process it with negative self-talk. Your self-talk gives meaning and "color" to the situation. You focus on the negative aspects, dwelling upon them and imagining all kinds of difficult resulting scenarios. You follow the process along until you are too scared, befuddled, and anxiety-ridden to think clearly about how to stop it.

The key is to stop the cycle, either at the point of when a trigger is about to set it off or once the negative self-talk begins.

Going Positive

The good news is that there is another option: learning positive self-talk. This kind of self-talk keeps you positive and focused. In many life circumstances, it can serve as a catalyst to help you deal with whatever situations come your way. At a minimum, it can give you strength, rest your weary mind, and build optimism that things are probably better than you thought them to be!

Identifying the Voices

Sometimes if you think about what the voices say to you, you can recognize their source. You may hear your father or mother, or your older sibling, or a past boss, or an ex-girlfriend or boyfriend. The words you use to tell yourself something might be familiar words that others have used either toward themselves or toward you. Certain ideas have had a big impact on you over the years. When you become attuned to the voices and what they say, there may be some familiar themes. Many times the interpretation people have of what's "good" or what's "bad" is really someone else's perspective that has become ingrained. Just as the key to negative self-talk lies in finding a positive self-talk, so you can fan the flames of your memory to remember good, positive things people have said to you.

"Batter Up!"

In the next chapter, you will have a chance to complete assessments specific to your life, and your reactions. But first let's look at the difference between positive and negative self-talk in more detail to understand how it actually writes a story in your life.

Think of listening to a ballpark broadcaster announcing a baseball game. Now imagine that the announcer hasn't actually seen the game yet. He is telling the audience what's happening *before the play has started*. "The next batter up is going to hit a home run. This crowd is going to go wild. The batter will run around the bases and experience a hamstring. He'll wonder whether he can finish without falling down. It's going to be an amazing event to watch!"

How much fun would that be for you if you were in the audience? Would you like to know what was going to happen before it happened? Most people would answer, "No!" The fun is in the anticipation, watching the game unfold. The fun is in not knowing how things will turn out.

Oddly enough, though, through your self-talk—whether good or bad—you live your life as if an announcer in your head is telling the plays before they happen. You tell yourself what things mean, what's going to happen next, what someone means by his mannerisms and facial expressions, whether the day is going to be good or bad, and on and on. You don't give yourself the chance to just experience life because the commentary is telling you what the experience is before you have it!

Writing the Story

Picture this, as best you can. It's a beautiful day. You leave your house and smell the air of spring. You had time to get ready this morning so you were not rushed and you feel good. You find yourself smiling as you walk down your front stairs. Your spirits are up, and it feels like a good day is ahead. Just as you step on the last step, a man comes running around the corner full force ahead. He seems to be staring directly at you. His long coat is flapping behind him as he runs and his face shows what you interpret to be some concern.

Stop here. It's possible that negative self-talk might be telling you to be scared or paranoid. Perhaps at some point in the past you've had a bad experience with a stranger. Maybe you were mugged or threatened by someone whom you met on the street. Because of that, your mind is whispering, "Is this guy a threat to me? Maybe he's going to grab me or hurt me." That sort of negative self-talk stems both from the situation and from your memories of similar situations. But you don't have to give in to it. Rather, tap into your positive self-talk:

"Wow, that guy is really going fast. I wish I could run like that. In fact, I'm so happy I started that exercise plan last week. I just noticed, in thinking about how in shape he is, that I am feeling much better about myself. I think I am getting toned already. I am going to find a few more times on my calendar to get more exercise. I always feel so good when I do. He is making me laugh with that funny face he has. I always have a similar expression when I am running to get in shape."

Which Is the "Right" Story?

So, which story is correct? Is the man a threat? Is he a danger to you? Or is he a reminder of things that you value and care about? Only you can answer those questions. But by shifting away from negative to positive self-talk, you create less anxiety and more opportunities for yourself.

Choose to Shift It

It's time to learn how to stop and shift your self-talk more positively. You can use self-talk to calm your anxious mind. It's about having choices. Until now you've had no choice—negative self-talk rules your day. But that's about to change.

Earlier you completed a number of assessments to identify the main sources of anxiety in your life. In the chapters that follow, you will learn how positive self-talk can be applied in a variety of circumstances.

Learning positive self-talk and the right words to say won't, by itself, change your life overnight. However, the more you can practice it and make it a habit, the more choices you will have. And the more you can learn to replace negative self-talk with positive self-talk, the more you'll be in control of your life. Positive self-talk builds and offers confidence and hope.

part II

CHAPTER 4

Building Your Self-Talk Toolbox

Are you ready for a calmer you? Are you ready for the steps you need to take to quell your anxiety, calm your mind, and allow yourself more positive options and outcomes in life? It really is up to you. It feels as though these things are out of your control, but the power is within you. By taking the assessments in Chapter 2 and using the steps in Chapter 3 to identify your triggers, you are already in a new state of awareness about the sources and impact of negative self-talk. You know it's created a more anxious you. But it's made promises that it can't keep. It has told you stories and given you endings without ever letting you have a chance to create a different outcome.

The beauty of positive self-talk is that you can call upon it during times of everyday anxiety and stress, or during times when things are spiraling out of control. The fact is, there *is* a calmer you. There is a you that can stand inside the tornado as it swirls around you and not get caught in the storm. If you are ready to make a life change and choose calm over anxious, it's time to uninvite the negative self-talk and invite in a more positive and powerful you. Taking the steps outlined in this book, learning more about your own cycles of negative self-talk, and examining the veracity of what these voices tell you are all critical pieces of the puzzle. But, you have to take some steps. You have to commit to a new way of being. You have to decide it's time to allow the calmer you to emerge.

Using Your Tools and Your Assessments

This book is not intended as a one-time read. It's meant to compel you to action and to give you steps, tools, and ways to move your negative states to more positive ones. You might believe that this world doesn't allow for a calm mind, and yet in the middle of the tornado, there are many people standing still and watching it pass by. You can do the same. In this chapter, you'll learn what tools you must keep in your positive self-talk toolbox to keep you calm and in control.

Commitment

The first thing is to make a commitment to yourself. Commit to a new you, a new approach.

Write your commitment on a 3" × 5" card or somewhere you can post it and see it often. Write it in the present tense and review it often. You might write something like: "I commit to a calmer me." Or "I am becoming calmer every day." Or "I take the steps I need to take to remove negative self-talk from my life."

Write the statement that works best for you here:

_____

_____

Your Personal Plan

If you haven't worked on any of the assessments, go back to Chapters 2 and 3 now. Start with the one in Chapter 2 so you can identify your specific areas of problems or weakness and then go on to the evaluation of triggers in Chapter 3. It is important to understand the areas in life that are major triggers for you. While most of life may present frustrations from time to time, some areas are more stress- and anxiety-inducing than others. For some people, their work life is great but they haven't met the person of their dreams, so they engage in negative self-talk when they get home feeling lonely and unwanted. Others find that anxiety permeates everything they do. Others have a terrible boss or difficult working situation—or can't find a job at all—and feel negative and depressed every time they think about work. Just remember, *you can't fix the problem until you know what the problem is.*

There are no right or wrong answers in the assessments. It's all about learning more about you and your anxiety. There is no benefit to ignoring what troubles you, or to pretending it will go away on its own. And, while this book can provide many guideposts to deal with anxiety and make different choices, you must first understand where your anxiety comes from, what triggers it, and what sends it into action. Then, you want to be aware of how it takes over, what it says to you, and the impact on your mind and body.

Keeping Track of Your Negative Self-Talk

Earlier I talked about using 3" × 5" cards to write down negative self-talk so you can learn how it runs amok and how to counter it. As well, I recommend that you get a journal and write things down. Some people are hesitant to do this, but it's very helpful. If you don't want to keep a journal, consider sending yourself a text message or keeping a note in your smartphone. Or you may want to jot ideas down on sticky notes and then post them where you can review them. Consider speaking into a small tape recorder that you carry with you when something occurs to you that would be helpful to remember. Whatever you choose to do, it is critical that you remind yourself to stay aware and uncover the negative self-talk. The more you can see clearly when and where it moves in, the more power you have to ask it to leave and replace it with positive self-talk. Simply using positive affirmations can be beneficial, but to really shift from anxiety to a calmer you, you have to identify the negative self-talk and make different choices about it.

Resolve here how you will capture your negative self-talk and identify it throughout the day. What method will you use to keep track of it?

_____

_____

Take note of the events that trigger you and note down your reaction to them each time you notice negative self-talk creeping in. And don't let your notes sit unremembered. Refer to them at least once per day to start to see if there are patterns or commonalities that occur.

The Next Steps

In addition to writing your commitment to make the change you want and identifying a method to keep track and become more aware of your self-talk, you will want to identify which sections of this book might be most useful for your immediate problems. After looking again at the table of contents, scan quickly to find those chapters that apply most to you. Then read them carefully. Find the steps that seem most appropriate for your situation, your lifestyle, and your needs. It may be helpful to copy these pages so you have them handy at all times. No real change happens without a plan. You must have a way to integrate what you are learning here into your day-to-day life or it can't become real for you.

Review the steps you will take the next time that negative self-talk creeps in. Write them down and keep them somewhere to which you have easy access. Perhaps you can keep a set next to your bed so you can repeat positive affirmations before bedtime. Keep a set in your pocket or your desk drawer at work. Don't stick them in a file—it's too easy to forget about them. Put them somewhere you can reach when you need them.

Next, schedule some time to work through the process you have identified. Some of the approaches in this book require you to sit quietly, do deep breathing, or repeat affirmations. You can practice these at any time. In fact, you *should* practice so these exercises become a habit for you when the negative self-talk visits and you catch it in the act! You want to be ready to turn to your positive approach. The more you practice this, and the more comfortable you feel with it, the easier it will be to do it.

As you read each of the following chapters, put the exercises and recommendations into your proverbial bag of tricks. Pick out the approaches that work for you. If you want to find a buddy, figure out a way to do this. It can be very helpful to have the reinforcement of another person in turning your self-talk around. If you are going to practice self-hypnosis, schedule this into your day. Don't wait for a right time to make things happen—instead, plan for it. Make it a part of your life.

Once you have your plan, put it in writing. Whether you have a planning notebook, use calendar software, or put everything in a smartphone, don't rely on memory alone to remind you of the time to do a self-talk exercise. Schedule it. Write it down.

Commit to it. Change won't happen without deliberate actions to make it happen.

Review, Modify, and Succeed

Instead of assuming that everything will work out fine now that you have a plan, take deliberate steps to review what's happening. Not everything works for every person. Some of the approaches might be great for your buddy or a friend who reads this book, but they might not work for you. The reason this book is packed with ideas and approaches is to give you the chance to find the one that fits who you are.

As you practice the approaches, pay attention to what's working and what's not. Again, it can be helpful to write some notes and capture thoughts. Each time you practice something, make a note of what it felt like. What didn't work that well? What did you like? What would you want to modify next time? Make this process about you—don't worry about the right and the wrong. Focus on what will work for you.

Be sure to capture the "Why?" Why didn't the approach work as well as you hoped? Why did one approach work better than another? What sorts of things affected the outcome? Then note what you might want to do differently. What might you change for next time? Are there pieces you could take from one approach and put with another?

Lastly, identify your best next steps. What things will you continue to commit to going forward? It can be helpful to state your commitment on a scale of 1–10. How committed are you to a calmer, more peaceful you?

Calm

It is possible to move from anxiety to a calmer you. The negative self-talk you have taken on has helped you to believe that it wasn't possible. You know now that there is a different option. You can be calm. You can feel good about yourself. You can feel good about your life. Commit to do so today. Walk through the steps outlined here. Don't take shortcuts. You deserve to be calm. You deserve a life without anxiety as an ever-present nag. Start to walk to that new life today.

CHAPTER 5

Anxiety in Personal Relationships

Relationships are in many ways both the key to our happiness and success and the bane of our existence. The people closest to us can support us and guide us throughout life, and they can also make our lives completely miserable. Many people haven't learned how to really be natural and positive in relationships. You may look to another person for your happiness and when he doesn't do what you expect, it makes you unhappy. You may blame people around you for the problems you have—your parents didn't give you the right support or your siblings have ignored you or friends have betrayed you. Anywhere human beings gather, there is the potential for problems.

Some people are well intentioned but awkward or self-destructive in how they act in a relationship. For example, Harry craves attention (a positive outcome), but he tries to get it by acting aggressively and causing scenes in public places (poor delivery). The result is precisely the opposite of what he wants—people avoid Harry in order not to be part of his destructive behavior, and as a result Harry doesn't get what he really needs.

Sometimes it seems as if there is always something amiss with our relationships. While things are going well with your spouse, you may be fighting with the neighbor. If your children are behaving, your mother-in-law is causing you trouble. These relationship problems are fueled by negative self-talk, which is often the third wheel in our relationships. Negative self-talk colors your reaction to and impression of other people in situations that range from dealing with conflict and anger in relationships to loss of a loved one to disappointments in life. This chapter will examine the different relationship scenarios that cause stress and anxiety and will look at the common self-talk people use. You'll do some exercises to examine your own self-talk and learn new positive ways of talking to yourself to help heal some of your broken relationships or broken feelings toward others.

Relationships Can Really Hurt

The research on how relationships can truly hurt is astounding. Negative self-talk and the resulting anxiety can actually drive people to hurt one another. Some studies have shown that close to 50 percent of the violent crimes against family members each year are committed against spouses. Every nine seconds in the United States, a woman is assaulted or beaten. Around the world, at least one in every three women has been beaten, coerced into sex, or otherwise abused during her lifetime. Most often, the abuser is a member of her own family. Domestic violence is the leading cause of injury to women—more than car accidents, muggings, and rapes combined. A mind led by negative self-talk doesn't "see" another person as valuable.

Problems in Relationships

Start by recognizing the immense web of relationships in which you're involved. There is your family of origin, including your parents and siblings and any extended family members such as aunts or uncles. You may be married, divorced, or in a committed partnership. You may have children. You probably have friends and colleagues with whom you interact on a regular basis. And in this age of social networking, relationships pervade our lives. We often spend hours online communicating, reading, and finding out information about other people.

When your relationships are good, they make you happy or positive about the world. A strong relationship can be a port in the storm of life. But when relationships sour or encounter difficulty, most people become fixated on the problems and use negative self-talk to bring themselves and other people down. Too much negative self-talk can turn feelings of love or attraction into hatred or disgust.

In other cases, you feel sadness or loss. Perhaps you are going through a divorce or have lost a loved one. It's common to experience depression and anxiety, overwhelmed by negative emotions. Rather than focusing on positive self-talk—remembering the good times you have had with your friend, relative, or spouse—you allow your negative self-talk to take over. "My life will never be full again. The loss is too great—the hole is too big." Or, "I'm too young to be alone, but I will be alone for the rest of my life."

I'm Not Happy, but I Don't Know How to Tell You

Behavioral research shows us that only about 18 percent of the population is comfortable with conflict. That leaves 82 percent trying to avoid conflict whenever possible; at best, they tolerate it when it comes their way. The problem is, some degree of conflict is inherent in relationships. It can be as small as your partner leaving the cap off the toothpaste in the bathroom, or as large as telling your spouse you don't want to have children when you previously said you were open to them!

In romantic relationships there are hundreds of opportunities each day for differences of opinion to surface. But of course, relationships aren't limited to romantic ones. There's the sibling who behaved inappropriately (at least, in your view) at the last family dinner. Or the child who responds to your rules with,

"I hate you!" Relationships are a regular stomping ground for conflict.

Some people are so attuned to conflict that even when a relationship is relatively harmonious, they wait anxiously for the other shoe to drop. You can adopt an attitude of avoiding conflict, hoping it will resolve itself, but as you've probably learned the hard way, that doesn't happen. Unresolved conflicts simmer and bubble just below the surface until they erupt again. For this reason, being able to deal constructively and positively with conflict in a relationship is an important skill.

Unhappily Married? You Are Not Alone!

Author Dana Adam Shapiro (*You Can Be Right (or You Can Be Married): Looking for Love in the Age of Divorce*), in an October 2012 interview with Buzzfeed.com, says, "I think 17 percent of marriages are happy. Fifty percent of marriages end, and of marriages that stay together, I think a third are happy, a third are happy enough, and a third are unhappy." Hmmm . . . Could negative self-talk be contributing to the unhappiness? It's worth giving positive self-talk a try!

Changing Your Self-Talk to Deal with Others

Given the crucial role relationships play in our lives, we need to counter negative self-talk that can pull them off track. Here's what you need to do.

Step One

Take the time to think about what you'd like in this relationship. What would the relationship look like if things were going as you'd like them to? What would the other person be doing or saying? How would you be interacting with him or her? What issues would you like to discuss with this person for a positive outcome? Make notes here about how you would like this relationship to be, and how you would like to be in this relationship. Be as clear as you can about what you really want.

_____

_____

Step Two

Now take a minute to sit quietly and imagine what it is like to feel confident and in a good place with regard to this relationship. It can be helpful to close your eyes and picture the positive feelings in any way you can. Not everyone "sees" pictures in their minds, and this is okay. Just imagine how you might feel and what you might think about the relationship. Imagine what the other person is doing in response to you. Is he listening more effectively? Are you resolving issues together?

Are you just having more fun? Run pictures, thoughts, feelings, or ideas through your mind about the positive outcome you desire for this relationship.

Step Three

Now practice positive self-talk. Read the following phrases and see which ones most fit you and your situation or which ones you can most relate to and seem the most "real" to you.

- "I deserve to have a good relationship."
- "Personal relationships are meant to be fulfilling, not draining."
- "It's important to bring up issues, concerns, thoughts, ideas, or whatever I want to talk about within my relationships."
- "I am confident in my relationship. Having a chance to talk about obstacles gives us a chance to fix them together."
- "I do not control the reaction of others. I can only control my own actions and reactions."
- "I stay focused on what I want out of this relationship, not on what's wrong."
- "Attitude is everything. I believe this relationship can work. I try to find new ways to do my part toward that end."

Step Four

Now put this all together. Find a place to sit quietly and close your eyes. Imagine this relationship is strong. Imagine that it is bringing you joy. Imagine that you are able to be real and feel good about yourself in this relationship. Get an idea in your mind about the next interaction with this person. See or believe that interaction will have a positive outcome. Look at the list above and choose the self-talk that will make these pictures real for you. Practice with these words and repeat them over and over again until they seem real to you. It's very important that you allow these words to sink in. The more you allow your mind to grasp ideas and images and words that make this relationship more positive and more fulfilling, the more your mind will help you work toward that end.

Step Five

As you work with this, remember to keep your journal or tape recorder close by. Observe your reactions to the person in the relationship. Note where you get triggered, and where you can bring your positive self-talk to bear. It's important to look at the process as ongoing so you can continue to reinforce the new, more positive approach.

Remember that no relationship will change overnight. People adopt certain actions and reactions in relationships, and it takes a while to embrace new behaviors on the part of someone you may be close to. You will need to be committed to plow through even when your negative self-talk tells you there is no point and nothing will change.

Dealing with Loss

You may have invested a lot in a relationship and cared about the other person; she may have cared about you. But then, for whatever reason, she left.

People leave relationships for many reasons. Everyone is on this earth on a temporary basis, so sooner or later we all leave as a result of death. But there are many other reasons relationships dissolve.

- More than 50 percent of marriages end in divorce; husbands and wives leave each other every day.
- People whom you trust or believe in can pick up and leave you, sometimes without warning or notice. Perhaps they move away because of a job change, or perhaps they want to make a change in their lives. The point is, they're not there anymore.
- People may leave a relationship emotionally. Sometimes the worst loneliness is having someone there, but feeling alone!
- People may leave you because of Alzheimer's or other mental incapacitation.

People may leave for a short time, and sometimes they leave forever. In both cases, it creates a feeling of loss, and loss is hard. The void left often feels large. Some days the pain and grief can become overwhelming. Negative self-talk enhances the feelings of grief. Your mind tells you that you will never feel okay again. The world will never be the same without the person you've lost. You may begin to think about your own mortality.

Grief is normal. Feeling a sense of loss and the void that follows is also normal. Never recovering from the grief or the loss is not okay. Grieving is natural, but you must find ways to deal with the grief. Negative self-talk and the ruminations associated with it can pull you in day by day. This is an especially crucial area in which you need positive self-talk to help you work through your grief and come to a better place.

Before you start the self-talk exercises in this section, be sure you have given yourself adequate time to grieve. What's a "normal" time? It differs for everyone, but if you are reading this section years after losing someone, you should work on this exercise.

When you lose someone you care about, it doesn't remove the person from your consciousness—this means you must eventually look at the loss differently. If, for example, you lost your spouse to an acrimonious divorce, constantly talking to yourself about him or her in a negative fashion isn't healthy for you. It isn't changing anything, and it isn't fixing anything. You need to get on the positive self-talk train.

Powerful Self-Talk to Replace Powerful Loss

This section will work if you feel ready to make some kind of life shift in this area. No one can tell you that you are ready; you must make that decision for yourself. Everyone grieves differently, and some people need more time than others. Pay attention to your needs.

Step One

Because you are dealing with a hole, a void, a loss of some kind, you may not know what success and a positive outcome looks like. You might only know that you don't want to continue in the kind of pain you're in. First, write down a few ideas about what the loss of this person means to you. Write both how the loss affects you and also how it makes you feel.

Losing this person impacted my life because

_____

_____

When I think about the loss of this person, I think about

_____

_____

My own self-image is impacted by the loss of this person because _____

_____

_____

I feel stuck in this loss because

_____

_____

Step Two

Review what you have written. Read all of these sections. Circle any words that stand out to you as high impact. In other words, what catches your attention when you read it? What really drags you down emotionally? Review your list of triggers from Chapter 3. Do any of these words relate back to these triggers?

Step Three

Now make a commitment to dealing with this loss in a different way. You've reached the end of your formal grieving process, and now you will "miss" the person in a different, hopefully healthier, way. Depending on the type of loss (i.e., death, divorce, a business partner who stole from you, a friend who dumped you, a sibling who moved away and never got in touch), you will close the loop differently. Here are some ways to do this. Choose one of these, or write one of your own.

- "I have given enough of my life over to grieving. I no longer want to devote energy to mourning this loss. It doesn't diminish the person's importance to me, but I need to move on with my life."

- "Losing someone is a natural life process. It hurts to suffer the loss, but it's normal. People leave in a variety of ways all of the time. I am not the only person to experience loss. I am ready to move into the next phase of my life and give up mourning this loss."

- "I was lucky to have _____ in my life. I will always miss him/her in some way, but my life is full and I intend to fill it even more. I am ready to find what the next phase has to offer me."

- "I'm done. I've grieved. I've suffered. I've mourned. I need to move on."

Review these statements, or write one of your own. It's important here to put something in writing that allows you to commit to a finality. Know that the person is gone. Allow yourself to fill the void that he or she left with something else. Make that commitment now in writing. _____

_____

Step Four

Now you need a plan to fill the void left by this person. Right now negative self-talk fuels this void, and it likely widens the emptiness. (If it doesn't widen the void, it certainly doesn't shrink it at all!) Loss results in a void that needs to be filled with something else. What steps can you take to begin to heal? Can you join a support group? Can you find a roommate? Can you locate someone else to be your partner? Can you take up a hobby? Can you go out with a friend? Can you volunteer at a nursing home? Can you donate your time to a child in need?

What steps can you take that will give you a focus, or something new to fill that void? Write any ideas that come to mind here:

_____

_____

Step Five

Now that you have committed to move past your grieving, have identified some of your fears about the transition, and have found some ways to fill that void, you are ready to begin integrating positive self-talk into the process. Positive self-talk here is critically important because you will need reinforcement and reminders over and over again of your commitment to move past this loss. Your positive self-talk should start first thing in the morning, and it should carry on throughout your day so that you are constantly reminding yourself of your desire to fill that void.

- "I loved/cared about/trusted/enjoyed (identify your emotion around this person) _____, but she/he is gone. I have mourned the loss, and now I look forward to finding what the next phase of my life will bring."
- "For every door that closes, another one opens. I believe this, and I keep my eyes peeled for the next opened door."
- "I am a fulfilled person of my own making. I don't need another person to fill me. I am okay on my own."
- "Everyone goes through what I am going through in one way or another. Loss is a part of life. I'm moving on."

- "Life holds all kinds of promise for me. I look forward to what's coming next. I live my life with hope."
- "The world is filled with people who need someone. I can be that person to someone else, and so I look around for opportunities to be a friend, a partner, or a supporter to someone else."
- "I have something to offer. I actively seek ways to share my time and talents with others."
- "Life is filled with promise and opportunity."

Step Six

Dealing with loss may require you to go back to any one of these steps over and over again. You must commit to finalizing your grief. You must commit to filling the emptiness. You must commit to finding positive self-talk that bolsters hope within you. Review these steps and return to any one where you feel stuck or stymied. And remember to use positive self-talk often and consistently.

Dealing with loss is difficult, but it is something that every human being has to face in one way or another. Grieving and mourning is natural and has its place. Allow yourself the space to mourn, but then make a decision that your anxious mind is done mourning and is ready to move into a new place. Most everything you will read in this book is about making a different decision. It's about letting go of the pain that causes your mind to run wild and to wreak havoc on your happiness. Loss provides a great opportunity to fall into a void and feel ill-equipped to pull yourself out of it. If you continue to struggle, you might want to review the steps in this section over and over to find the places you most need to focus on. Realizing you have a choice is the first important step, but it's necessary to keep practicing these steps until that choice becomes a reality.

CASE STUDY

Let's look at someone dealing not with loss but with disappointment in a relationship. This is really only one step removed from dealing with loss. Like loss, the type of disappointment can be minor or severe, but your ability to move past it and heal the relationship and yourself should not depend on the severity of the issue.

Louise was married for almost thirty years to a man she met shortly after graduating from college. Both of them had productive careers, and they had two children who grew up, married, and moved away from home. Louise was looking forward to a peaceful middle age and retirement. Until, that is, she found out that her husband had been unfaithful. He had a long-time mistress, with whom he'd had a child. Frank announced to her that he was leaving her to go live with his mistress.

Like many people whose trust in someone has been misplaced, Louise's first reaction was to beat up on herself. "How could I have been so blind?" she moaned. "Why was

I so stupid as to trust Frank? What's wrong with me that I didn't recognize for all those years that he's a pathological liar?"

Disappointment can bring heartache—and actual physical symptoms. Louise stopped eating well. She couldn't sleep, and she felt listless and without energy. As is common in such cases, Louise reinforced her loss through negative self-talk, which only deepened the heartache. Her anxiety and stress levels went through the roof. She wondered if she could ever trust someone—*anyone*—again.

Louise's disappointment is normal. Most people go into a relationship with some level of expectation. A spouse "should" do certain things for the other spouse; a friend "should" be trustworthy and kind; a parent "should" consider the best interests of the children before his own; and on and on and on. It's not that these "shoulds" are not true, but they are a judgment that one person makes about another. In fact, if these expectations were universally true, people would seldom disappoint in relationships.

Frank's views about how he "should" handle himself in a relationship were different from those held by Louise. This disagreement is what led to crisis and disappointment. Frank honestly believed that cheating was a normal part of marriage; his father had been constantly unfaithful to his mother, but their marriage had lasted. Louise set an expectation in her relationship without Frank knowing it was there (though we can certainly say he *should* have known, since marital infidelity is not a recipe for a happy marriage).

Positive self-talk can be very powerful in relationships, strengthening them before a disappointment happens or helping a person to heal after the disappointment. That proved true in this case. After visiting a counselor and taking some time to recover from her original shock, Louise was able to turn her self-talk around. At her therapist's advice, she wrote down her thoughts in a journal.

She started by focusing on the marriage and thinking about her expectations for it. She wanted Frank to be a good provider; a warm, loving companion; and a faithful spouse. Not surprisingly, when she did this, in one part of her mind she said, "This is stupid. Of course a spouse *should* be faithful. That isn't my expectation; that's what our vows said." But something went wrong—and Frank didn't live up to those vows. So Louise realized that in any future relationship, she would have to spell out clearly that she needed her partner to be faithful.

Next, Louise thought about how Frank disappointed her. Though it was difficult, she tried to refrain from judgmental language and just wrote down the facts of what happened. Being as factual as possible helped remove some of the emotional sting from the disappointment.

Then Louise thought about what she wanted from this exercise. Did she want to forgive Frank? To heal the relationship? Rather than pick a negative outcome, which she might have done before ("I want to make him and his little bimbo pay!"), she concluded, "I want to move past this and have a warm, loving, trusting relationship in the future. And I want to forgive Frank but make it clear that he is no longer a central part of my life."

Now Louise went to work on her positive self-talk. She realized that the success of positive self-talk in this situation depended entirely on her willingness to approach Frank differently and have an attitude of healing, forgiveness, and positive energy.

She wrote down a list of positive self-talk options to see which ones resonated most with her.

- "Everyone is human. Humans make mistakes. I wanted a healthy relationship with Frank, but I know I've moved on from him. I choose to focus on what's good in my life."

- "I have made mistakes. I have things in my life I would like to do over. I freely offer Frank my forgiveness for the future."

- "I want to be emotionally and physically healthy. Harboring resentment isn't good for anyone—I focus on the positive aspects of this and other relationships."

- "I freely let go of Frank. It is no longer meant to be a relationship in my life."

- "I get stronger every day. I learn from every situation and every relationship. I choose to learn."

- "Problems in my relationships give me a chance to look at me. I want to be a better friend and mother, a better person."
- "I do everything possible to keep this relationship healthy."
- "Being healthy in future relationships is important to me. I strive toward health and shake off those things that bring me down."

Finally, Louise used visualization and positive imaging to remember Frank as she first met him. She did not offer judgment; she recognized that many things had made him the person he was. She could not be with him, and it was time to move on.

As you go through your exercises, patterned on the ones outlined in the above case study, find a quiet place that you can sit uninterrupted. Have your positive self-talk affirmations with you so you can repeat them over and over again. Read these instructions first and once you know what to do, sit quietly and close your eyes. You will want to use as many senses as possible to picture or imagine or think about the other person and your desired outcome with him. First, picture the person in your mind. If you begin to associate anything negative, picture that person as a child in need. Picture that person as sad or scared or anything that makes him more vulnerable and accessible. Picture that person hurting in some way. Next, imagine you are there to embrace that person as he says "I'm sorry" over and over and over again. You may never hear the words from the person in real life, but you can hear them in this picture. The person is humbled and seeking support and forgiveness. Offer the person forgiveness now and, in your mind, tell him you are moving on.

Next integrate your self-talk. Take a phrase or two from the list in the case study above, or make up positive self-talk of your own, and use this language as your mantra over and over again as you sit quietly. Continue to repeat this self-talk until you feel your own anxiety and resentment toward the person diminishing.

Realize that the disappointment or resentment you hold toward someone is more hurtful to you than the other person. Most of the time other people don't feel our anger and resentment the way we want them to. In fact, they may become defensive or combative in reaction to your resentment. While your anxious mind ruminates over what's gone wrong, the other person is thinking that you are the problem. Using positive self-talk here and changing the dynamic of the conversation is good for you personally, as well as for your relationship.

Practice, Practice, Practice!

Relationships are challenging. They can bring out the best in people, as well as the worst. Even after you apply some of the positive self-talk methods in this chapter, another relationship will come along to challenge you. The exercises in this chapter are meant to be used over and over. Pick the self-talk that best fits your situation. Deal with relationships one at a time until you feel confident and more in control. Too many people want to be "right" in relationships. They don't want to cut the other person a break at all or give in to something. Instead, think of relationships as learning experiences—you learn about yourself and your triggers and reactions. You can guide a relationship using the positive self-talk you are learning. This process is about choice. It's about choosing mental health over an anxious mind. Keep choosing the approach that gives you more options and confidence.

CHAPTER 6

Anxiety in the Workplace

Work-related anxiety is far too common in our society. Think of the many things that can go wrong in one's job situation—difficult bosses, unreasonable expectations, too much responsibility for too little authority, too much work and not enough time to complete it, looming layoffs or RIFs (reductions in force), and generally terrible work conditions. But here again, you can turn the situation around and make work a place in which you find energy and purpose.

Most people spend a majority of their time at work. For many people their work is a big part of who they are. They identify their self-worth with their work. Others work just to survive. The truth is that since it occupies eight to fourteen hours of every day, five days a week, work can't help but permeate your life. It's precisely for this reason that it's time you took charge of your self-talk and changed your work situation. You don't have to get a new job; you can stay at the same place, but talk differently to yourself about it.

Of course, it's possible that you're reading this chapter because you *are* looking for a new job. You may have a lot of negative self-talk associated with your value in today's economy or your reputation from a past employer. Whatever the association with work and the reason for reading this chapter, you can take a different approach. In this chapter we'll look at a variety of common work situations. You will see the common negative self-talk that people use and learn ways to shift the negative self-talk to something more positive and powerful. Having tools to cope with the problems you encounter and the negative things you want to change is imperative.

Anxiously Seeking a Job

Job hunting is one of the more anxiety-arousing experiences people have in life. If you are someone out of work, you may need a job badly. If you are in a difficult work situation, you may feel a sense of urgency to change your circumstances and find a new situation. Perhaps you are a college student who has finished school with a great deal of debt, and the payments are starting soon. Or you may be an older person who devoted a career to a company only to find yourself out of work and not knowing what to do next.

Did you ever think about why job hunting is so unappealing? Rather than the excitement of a new opportunity, or the learning experience that comes from interviewing and talking to new people, most people categorize job hunting as a stressor. You won't hear many people saying, "I can't wait to embark on the job-hunt process!" Or, "I just love the rejections I get when I am job hunting!" *Most of the time it is unappealing because of the way people talk to themselves about it.*

The funny thing is, people usually like the experience of actually landing the new job. They just don't embrace the path to get there with enthusiasm and excitement!

If you are job hunting now, or believe you could be in the future, study this chapter to find ways to turn your self-talk from negative to positive. As a result, you'll experience job hunting in a different light.

Job Hunting Misconceptions

Nobody likes to be judged. But that's exactly what you tell yourself the interviewer or Human Resources person is doing as they look at your resume. If you submit a resume, make a phone call, or reply to a job posting and are not picked to move forward in the interview process, your self-talk might be something like this: "I don't have the skills necessary anymore. I'm obsolete. I might never find another job." Your negative self-talk might be about you and your capability. You might think, "Everyone else has an easy time finding a job. I'm just not good at this." Or you might say, concerning the potential employer, "What was I thinking sending my resume in to those jerks? I have heard they are rude and nonresponsive. I guess everything I've heard about them is true." Or it might be about the economy in general:"Things are so bad all around. No one is getting a job. The world is going to pot, and I'll probably never work again."

The Role of Negative Self-Talk

Sometimes, as we've said earlier, negative self-talk is used to beat up on yourself, but sometimes you might believe it will protect you from being hurt. If you can speak to yourself negatively about the company or person who interviewed you, then the problem (as your mind rationalizes it) really isn't about you. This is the fascinating thing about self-talk: It can change so you always have an excuse for why it is there and why it has the power to hurt you. You may even subconsciously enjoy its company. And all the while it is raising your anxiety levels and unsettling your mind.

There are opportunities to use more positive self-talk to change your attitude going into a situation, and perhaps to steer the outcome more positively, too. Positive self-talk will allow you to face the situation squarely instead of pulling the covers over your head and staying in bed. Job hunting can be difficult, but positive self-talk gives you a tool with which to counter that difficulty.

If you are in a job hunt right now, complete the following assessment. This will allow you to establish your current state, or current views on the job-hunt process, so you can identify which parts are most difficult for you:

I know the type of job I am looking for and where I would be a good fit	Y/N
I present myself confidently in interviews	Y/N
I look forward to interviews and meeting new people	Y/N
I consider the interview process to be easy for me	Y/N
I realize that the interviewer may not be objective, but this doesn't reflect on me	Y/N
I believe that things happen for a reason so if I don't get a job, something else is waiting	Y/N
I think my resume is solid and I describe my background well	Y/N
I feel good about my capabilities and this comes through in interviews	Y/N

Now review this list. Did you answer "no" to any of these statements? Which ones? Circle any of the sentences to which you responded "no." Now in the section below, write a couple of sentences about your self-talk that relates to these statements. What might you say to yourself about this aspect of job hunting?

For example, if you said "no" to "I consider the interview process to be easy for me," you might write that your self-talk says something like this: "Interviewing is really hard. I never come across well in interviews. I always feel like the interviewer is waiting for me to make a mistake. Interviews are a stupid way to choose employees anyway; there should be more emphasis put on looking at someone's background on the resume."

Review the entire list. Identify all of the areas where you answered "no" and fill in the following with your possible self-talk related to each.

Category from the list _____. What self-talk I have related to this area of the job search _____

_____

Category from the list _____. What self-talk I have related to this area of the job search _____

_____

Category from the list _____. What self-talk I have related to this area of the job search _____

_____

Category from the list _____. What self-talk I have related to this area of the job search _____

_____

Get Into the Scene

It can be helpful to sit down, close your eyes, and picture yourself to the best of your ability in this type of situation as it might unfold. "See," think, or feel what it was like the last time you went on an interview or were preparing for one. As you create the experience in your mind, become aware of your self-talk related to it. Get as many elements as possible in your mind that make you think and feel about the situation. Just thinking about the experience may set your negative self-talk in motion. Capture any "talk" related to the experience now.

_____

_____

_____

_____

The Self-Talk You Encounter

Now write down your negative self-talk associated with the situations here. What do you think? How do you feel? What words do you use to explain the results you expect? Spend a few minutes exploring your personal self-talk.

_____

_____

Be honest with yourself about what you say and what you believe. Minimizing it or trying to explain it away isn't helpful as you pursue a positive change. You must be brutally honest about what you think, the words you use, and how the negative self-talk creeps in and interprets the situation.

Turning It All Around

Once you are clear on the negative ways you self-talk, you're ready to create positive self-talk and unfold a different set of expectations related to the job hunt. Think of this as rewriting the script. I hope at this point you've realized that self-talk is only made-up stories in your mind. You might believe them to be true and argue that they are fact-based or based on real experiences, but what's happening is that you are using negative self-talk to make predictions. You are giving the play-by-play from the announcer's box before the play has happened. You are telling a story that may, or may not, be true.

The next step to begin to turn this around, and have more energy and confidence in your job-hunt process, is to tell a different story. Once you are willing to acknowledge that you make up the commentary that plays in your mind, you can acknowledge that the commentary is malleable. You can shape it, and create it, in any way you determine.

The Step-by-Step Process

First, take the time to think about the interview or job-hunt process. If you have been at it for a while, or have had generally bad luck in the past, you have a reaction to it, most probably negative. You then become anxious about what might happen to you. You talk to yourself about the expected negativity. You then might encounter more negative experiences to "prove" to yourself you were right. Your negative experiences pile up, and you become ill-equipped to deal effectively with a job hunt or interview. You can find data and facts to support whatever belief system you hold. If your beliefs are negative, your mind will be drawn to those circumstances that confirm the negativity.

In fact, each situation has a flip side—the good in life has some negativity contained within, and the bad in life has some positive aspects associated with it. In this exercise, you're going to turn your mind toward the positive stuff. When anxiety rules the day and negative self-talk compounds it, the window to the world is mostly negative as confirmation. Bringing a positive attitude is critical to coping with life in a more balanced fashion.

Let's change the plays in the step-by-step process.

Step One

Clear your mind of any past experiences or thoughts about your job hunt. It's really important to push out of your mind any negative connections. Your mind should be a blank canvas, and you should be painting the picture on it in whatever colors you choose. Once your mind is cleared, use that space to focus on what you want with regard to the next step in finding a job. What does success look like to you? What kind of job would suit you well? What would make you happy in the job-hunting process? Capture those things that would make you happy or bring you joy. Be as clear and specific as possible. It's important to be clear about where you want to head and what success will look like to you once you get there. Take your time writing these down. Writing things down is important because it allows the mind to take a mental picture of what you want. It becomes more concrete and more believable when you see it in writing.

_____

_____

_____

_____

_____

Step Two

Now do your best to imagine a successful outcome. Imagine yourself in your job-hunt process, sending out resumes and going on interviews. Sit up confidently as you imagine this. Smile and take on the aura of someone who is happy and successful in this area. This might require closing your eyes and sitting quietly. Imagine how you will feel with a successful outcome. See yourself enjoying the process, talking to the interviewer in a confident manner, taking a rejection letter in stride, and posting your resume with enthusiasm and commitment. See yourself, or think about, networking and talking to others in an upbeat and positive fashion. See the positive outcome that you desire and have written about for this process. Take all the time you need to do this, until this picture feels or seems real to you.

Step Three

Now practice positive self-talk. Choose from the following positive statements the ones that most resonate with you. If you don't see a statement that you like, use these as a guideline to write your own.

- "I am just as capable as anyone else in interviews and in the job-hunting process."
- "I have had past successes that I draw upon to be more successful as I search for my next job. My past successes include _____

_____

_____."

- "Job hunting is something everyone has to do at some point in her or his life. My experience is no different than millions of other people—it's really no big deal. Everyone gets through it."
- "I know the right job is out there for me, and I am confident I am going to be led, or will lead myself, to find it."
- "The person reading my resume or interviewing me is just another human being. He has hopes and fears like anyone else. He doesn't control my life or my feelings about myself."
- "I learn something from every interview I go on, every resume I send, and every conversation I have in the job-hunt process. I look at it as a learning experience."
- "I am resilient and able to keep going even if things initially don't go as I would like them to."

Step Four

Now put this all together. Again, you will find a place to sit quietly and close your eyes. Imagine you are reaching the job-hunting goals you have set. You see yourself clearly doing what you need to do. Now use the self-talk above and repeat the words over and over again. It's very important you allow yourself to let these words sink in. Remember you are telling yourself a story. You have the power to talk about how this story will unfold. You are writing a script, but the play has not begun. You are the director, the producer, and the actor. Choose the script carefully and believe in the outcome.

As you go through the job-hunt process, you may want to do this exercise several times a day. Each time you face defeat, turn to one of the positive self-talk statements that help you cope with it. As you prepare for an interview, sit quietly and picture the positive outcome you want as you say your positive self-talk silently to yourself. Say the self-talk out loud in the car as you drive to the interview. Run the messages as many times as you can, in a believable and confident manner. Remember that you are writing your own script. Choose the story lines wisely.

CASE STUDY

Let's see how this process of positive self-talk might play out for someone looking for a job.

Angie is a thirty-eight-year-old salesperson. For the past six years, she's been employed by a software firm, but a month ago she was laid off. Angie's thinking has been dominated by negative self-talk: I'm too old to start again; I can't stand rejection; the industry's changing too fast, and it's hard to keep up; a new job might mean moving to a new city, and I don't want to move. However, by moving from negativity to positive self-talk, she can start to turn things around, understand the possibilities for future employment, and prepare herself for a productive and successful job search.

The first thing Angie does is put aside her feelings of inadequacy, anger, and resentment. Now she starts from a clean beginning:

Step One

1. **What does success look like?** To Angie, success means *financial stability* so she can pay her bills and put money by for retirement; *career growth*, since she doesn't want to be stuck in the same job forever; and *personal fulfillment*, meaning the job should be interesting. She wants a culture where she has the chance to *add value and be successful* and where she can stay planted for a few years to come.

2. **What kind of job will suit her?** A well-paying job, which means starting in the middle instead of at the bottom of the career ladder; a job in the company with a long-term future; and, since Angie wants challenges, a job that includes some travel, although

she doesn't want to move to a new city at the moment.

3. **What would make her happy in the job-hunting process?** Angie understands (through her positive self-talk) that some rejection is inevitable in a job hunt. But she wants to get some leads and have some of those leads turn into interviews. She wants to know she's being taken seriously as a potential employee. Because she is in sales, she wants to make connections and network as she moves through the interview process. And, of course, ultimately she wants to find the right job for her.

Step Two

1. **Networking.** Angie thinks about networking online to get leads and post her resume, carefully considering what parts of her experience to emphasize for each job to which she applies.

2. **Interviewing.** Now she thinks about the interviews themselves. She sees herself: poised, professionally dressed, confident, answering the interviewer's questions. In some cases, she can imagine the interviewer will tell her that they've selected another candidate, but she sees herself accepting that news and moving on to the next interview.

3. **Succeeding.** Now Angie thinks about what it will be like when she gets that offer. She imagines herself sitting in an office across the desk from a manager

who's saying, "Angie, our company can use talent like yours. You have a lot to offer, and I look forward to working with you." Angie imagines telling her friends about the great job she's just landed and breaking the news to her family.

As this positive self-talk runs through her mind, Angie finds that she's sitting up straighter and that she's smiling.

Step Three

Now Angie's going to practice positive self-talk. She chooses the following positive statements as the ones that most resonate with her.

- "I am just as capable as anyone else in interviews and in the job-hunting process."
- "Job hunting is something everyone has to do at some point in her or his life. My experience is no different than millions of other people—it's really no big deal. Everyone gets through it."
- "I know the right job is out there for me, and I am confident I am going to be led, or will lead myself, to find it."

Step Four

Now Angie puts this all together. She sits in a calm, quiet place and closes her eyes. She imagines that she's reaching the job-hunting goals she's set. She sees herself doing what she needs to do. Now she repeats the phrases from Step Three. Every morning, before she starts her job search, she goes through this exercise. As a result, she finds she is more confident in interviews and more positive about the search's eventual outcome; thus, she feels her anxiety slowly fade away.

In the end it still takes Angie some time to find a job. She goes through some hard times. But with her self-talk turned from negative to positive, she is able to project a better attitude, one filled with confidence. And that impresses a company enough that they hire her to a good position with a salary to match. And because Angie projected an air of confidence throughout her job search, she has met many other people along the way who want to stay in touch with her. She may have set herself up for a future opportunity, too.

Dealing with the Difficult Ones on the Job

There aren't many people who haven't had a difficult boss or difficult coworkers at some point in their job lives. Sometimes a boss lets power go to his head and can cause disruption as a result. Sometimes coworkers relive their seventh-grade bully experience and lash out at you for no good reason. There are multiple situations where the workplace causes anxiety because the people in it are wreaking havoc. They limit your ability to be successful and even, in some cases, can cause you to lash out or get depressed, creating additional problems for yourself.

It's important to understand that you can't change others. The only actions and reactions you can control are your own. No matter what negative self-talk tells you, that remains true.

Change the Self-Talk, Change the People

Instead of waiting for some unforeseeable point when others will change, it's time to take the process into your own hands. This doesn't mean lashing out at work or hurting someone in your workplace to get satisfaction and revenge. Instead it means changing the tapes or the messages you are playing in your mind about your workplace and the people there. The voice that comes in to tell you how awful things are is not your friend. And you need to show it the door.

Because understanding how negative self-talk impacts us is a necessary first step, listen to what your self-talk tells you about your boss, your coworkers, or the difficult people you encounter at work. It could be customers who make your stomach churn or vendors who berate and upset you. Identify those with whom you have the problem and determine what problem you have with them.

Step One

Identify the difficult person here _____. If you have difficulty with multiple people in your workplace, you may want to do this exercise a number of times.

Step Two

Write some words about this person (or these people). What do you think about him/her? What words do you use to describe him/her in your mind? Bring the negative self-talk you have about him/her to the surface now.

_____

_____

Be honest with your thoughts. Don't sugarcoat and don't minimize. If you have strong feelings, write them. The feelings are sufficiently strong that they are having an impact on you, so write them down. Capture anything that bothers you, troubles you, or annoys you about this person.

Bringing in Positive Self-Talk

Remember that self-talk is like the announcer who is calling out the plays before they have even happened. In the case of a difficult person at work, you have likely had a real experience that initiated and fueled your negative self-talk. The person probably did something to you, treated you a certain way, or behaved in a manner that was distasteful. That's real. But now, because you connect this person with this experience, subconsciously you may believe that every time you interact with the person you will get the same result.

Unfortunately your negative self-talk may, in fact, be helping this to happen. You have an expectation, based on some past experience, and on that basis you predict what will happen in the future. Since your objective is to enjoy your work, feel good about going to your workplace, and have strong relationships with others, this negative attitude is a bad thing. So let's turn it around.

Step One

Acknowledge that you have had a bad experience with the person on whom you are focusing. In the space here, write why that person might have behaved in that way or treated you the way she or he did. Don't judge; just record the facts. Instead of saying, "My boss is a jerk and doesn't care about people," you might say, "My boss has a hard time managing communication when he/she is upset. He/she often comes off as angry and scary." You aren't excusing the behavior; you are just relabeling it without the negative emotion so that you can have more options in dealing with the person effectively. It's not "okay" for a boss to yell and humiliate people, and it's not "okay" for your customer to be sexually inappropriate. But a judgmental interpretation of these situations makes it more difficult for you to cope. You want to deal with the person in a different manner altogether.

Write here what the behavior is or what the situation entails and force yourself to think about it objectively. Take your time to capture as objectively as possible what's happening with this individual. You may want to do this in two steps.

Write the behavior you observe here:

_____

_____

_____

_____

_____

Now rewrite it as objectively and factually as possible with no judgmental or labeling words:

_____

_____

_____

_____

_____

It's about Choices

When dealing with difficult people in the workplace differently, you are not excusing disrespectful or damaging communication and behavior. Instead, you are giving yourself options to deal with someone. If the situation is untenable, you always have the choice to quit the job. If your negative self-talk tells you that isn't an option, practice positive self-talk instead and refer back to the section on job hunting to bolster your confidence!

Step Two

Choose some options for positive self-talk regarding this person.

Before you deal with the person next, spend some time practicing with some of the following language. It's helpful to review what you wrote about the person's actions and frame him or her in an objective, nonjudgmental light. Try to remove the sting that this person gives you. Your anxious mind is already putting this person in a box with a preset reaction on your part. Get this person out of the box and look at him or her in a different light. Again, you are not excusing bad behavior; in fact you're taking steps to protect your mind from toxic people. At a minimum you are getting a chance to move back and be more objective. Review the following list and choose some of the following language when you talk to yourself about the person.

- "Sometimes a stressful job situation brings out the worst in someone. Rather than respond negatively, I want to understand what's happening with this person. I practice compassion and understanding whenever possible."
- "This person does not rule my life. I rule my life. I can be courteous and professional, and I do not have to be afraid of anyone."

- "I make my own choices about how to interact with someone. If I decide I want to like this person, I can do so. I want my relationships to be effective and fulfilling."
- "Work is just work. It isn't the be-all and end-all in my life. I need to do a good job for my employer, but I don't need to expend all kinds of emotional energy over the people I work with."
- "There are always worse bosses, worse coworkers, and worse job situations out there. Today I am going to focus on finding the positive things associated with my work."
- "I am assertive and confident in my dealings with others. I set boundaries and am clear about what I need."
- "I find myself dealing with others at work more and more effectively all of the time. I view them in an objective fashion, and I seek to understand."
- "I surround myself with positive people at work whenever possible. I seek the company of those people who can help me, encourage me, or make the workplace more fun and enjoyable for me."

Action—Reaction: The Vicious Cycle

Sometimes if you have a different attitude when you approach someone, you receive a different response from her or him. Often we become stuck in a pattern of approach and response, approach and response; neither party will deviate from his or her script. For this reason, sometimes simply changing your approach will change the other person's response. At a minimum, it will allow you to see the situation differently. Changing anything in life from the normal unconscious responses you have to more deliberate conscious ones gives you a chance at a different view.

Step Three

Now put this all together. First go back and review the way you talked about this person, using the objective language from Step One. If you see anything that is judgmental, remove those comments. Use this as a chance to practice compassion and get into another person's proverbial shoes. Most people who engage in negative behavior are hurting somehow. The person you're interacting with may be seeking something positive. The boss who yells is sometimes really afraid of being seen as a phony. The coworker who doesn't hold up her end of the project commitments might lack the knowledge to complete her job successfully. The customer who swears at you might be in the midst of a personal crisis. Understanding this can often help you look beneath the outward behavior to get at the root cause. And in many cases, you might have been in their place in a prior situation. You may have acted it out differently, but you can probably relate to the pain they are trying to avoid or the fear they may feel that is driving their actions.

Step Four

Prepare for the next interaction with this individual by reading and rereading some of the positive self-talk about the interaction. Remember that if the positive self-talk listed in this section doesn't fit you, you can write your own. Be objective and positive.

If you genuinely want to shift this relationship, be genuine in your comments. Approach the person more openly and willingly, while expecting a positive outcome. Acknowledge that you are tired from the anxiety generated by the situation at your workplace. Commit to a change.

Keep repeating the cycle until it sticks. The next time the person engages in the behavior that triggers you, rather than beating up on yourself, realize that this is a process. Take out your positive self-talk and remind yourself of your goals in working with this person. This is for you. It's to calm your anxious mind.

Resistance to Negative Feedback or Workplace Conflict

Behavioral research has proven that only about 18 percent of the population has a core tendency toward conflict. They like to disagree or argue. They enjoy telling someone what's wrong or what they don't like. That leaves about 82 percent disliking conflict, trying to avoid it—often at all costs.

Unfortunately, in most work situations conflict is a fact of life. You, as supervisor or manager, may have to deliver bad news. You may need to give negative feedback to a colleague or subordinate. Or, perhaps, you're the one receiving the negative feedback. Perhaps a performance evaluation didn't go as you had hoped, and you learned your employer is unhappy with you.

Conflict in the workplace can be anxiety-inducing for many people. Thinking about the interaction beforehand and ruminating about it afterward provide your negative self-talk with lots to draw from! So learning to deal with conflict effectively is a critical job-related skill. Here again, the key is changing your self-talk from negative to positive.

Just Say What You Mean

There are many reasons people avoid conflict. Some people want to be liked. Some are afraid the volatility of the person they're interacting with will spark a conflict. Some don't know what words to use and may vacillate from over-aggressive in their comments to overly nice and unclear. It may feel easier to say "If I ignore the situation, it will just go away" or "Nothing is going to change anyway so what difference does it make?" In fact, this will make the potential for conflict worse.

At some point the situation will force you to address it. The benefit to learning positive self-talk as a tool to resolve conflict is that most people feel much better once they have been able to address a problem, receive criticism, and then move on.

Learning to Deal Effectively with Conflict

If you have determined this is an area of focus to you, let's walk through the steps to using positive self-talk to deal with conflict.

Step One

First you want to identify your triggers, the reactions you have to conflict-inducing, or potentially conflict-inducing, situations. What causes you to feel worry, anxiety, or fear with regard to conflict? What happens to you when you are faced with a conflict? Do you lie awake at night? Do you get sweaty palms or cold feet? Do you call in sick to work so you don't have to deal with it? Note here the situations that arouse anxiety in you, and how you react to them. Take your time to think about this so you can capture as many details as possible. If you aren't in a conflict-inducing situation right now, think about one from your past. Think about how you react, what your mind and body do to you in response to the conflict or thinking about the conflict. Be as clear as possible and capture as much as you can. The more you capture in writing, the easier it becomes to recognize such a situation the next time.

_____

_____

_____

Step Two

Now think about your negative self-talk. What is it about dealing with conflict or facing criticism that bothers you? What language do you use to talk to yourself about it? You might think it's obvious what people would say in these conflict situations, but don't make this assumption. Be clear about the negative self-talk and list words you use here.

_____

_____

_____

Step Three

Now, after you read the instructions for this next step, sit quietly for a minute and close your eyes. Get a picture in your mind of the positive outcome you desire. What would you like to happen in this situation? If you need to give negative feedback to a coworker, for instance, would you like her to smile and nod and accept your criticism? If you anticipate receiving negative feedback in a performance review, would you like to be able to sit confidently and listen to your boss in an understanding fashion? Would you like to be more objective about the situation? Whatever you want as an outcome that's different from what has happened in the past, spend some time picturing it now. Feel, think, and imagine how differently you will feel once you approach conflict with more confidence. Do this until you begin to realize that this outcome can materialize for you.

Step Four

Now, practice with positive self-talk. Use some, or all, of the following or make up some of your own that reinforce your ability to deal with the conflict and have a successful outcome.

- "Conflict is a fact of life. People deal with issues all of the time. I can deal professionally with whatever comes my way."

- "I am an adult. I'm not a child. Being bullied or yelled at doesn't affect me. I realize it is the other person's problem, not mine. Rather than get defensive, I seek to understand what's going on with that person."

- "Giving and getting negative feedback or criticism only allows a person to improve. If I don't know what's wrong, or I don't tell others what's wrong, how can anyone change? It's important to be honest."

- "Some people don't mature, and it shows in the workplace. I handle myself as an adult and let the behavior I dislike in others just roll off of me."

- "Sharing and receiving negative feedback is important. The issues won't go away, and when they are raised, they can be dealt with. There is nothing worse than having something simmer and then explode. I'd rather get it over with and move on to the next thing."

- "Work is work. There are more important things to be upset about in life. I have an objective view on work. I don't let it emotionally carry me away."

If it is helpful, you can use self-talk about a specific person or situation. Fill in the blank here with the name or names of people you want to deal with differently.

"_____ is just a person. He/she gets up every day just like I do and might even want to do a good job. Being afraid/fearful/resentful of _____ is silly. I'm a grown up and in charge of my actions and reactions."

Practice these self-talk options until you find the one or ones that fit you best. It can be helpful to imagine your positive outcome and repeat some of these self-talk affirmations while you do it. Reinforce and reinforce until you can own this positive approach to conflict resolution.

Remember that you are making a different choice. Right now the conflict is ruling you. The fear of it, the negative tapes you play as a result of it, the anticipation of it, is limiting your ability to be effective. You can manage it differently using this process and the positive self-talk. The conflict itself is less important than the story you tell yourself about it. Negative stories allow conflict to grow and flourish. Tell yourself different stories and experience a different outcome.

Overcoming the Fear of Public Speaking

In order to advance in many jobs, you must speak confidently in front of groups of people. At a minimum, in order to present your case about something, you have to know how to speak clearly, confidently, and in a manner that inspires confidence in others. Public speaking is one of the top fears among people in our society. The idea of getting up in front of a room and delivering a message can scare the dickens out of many people. You might picture yourself forgetting what you are supposed to say, falling off the stage, or having people stare at you blankly with a lack of interest or, even worse, disgust. The negative self-talk kicks in, and you become more and more anxious. By the time you speak, your palms are sweaty, your heart is racing, and your stomach is in turmoil.

You may not have a job in which you are required to speak in front of people, but mastering this skill opens doors and opportunities that might otherwise be closed to you. You may, in the future, be asked to state your feelings or ideas about something to a large group. It could be a town or neighborhood meeting where you take the microphone, or a school board meeting at which you want to speak out on behalf of your child. It could be a function where you make a toast to someone you care about. There are many life scenarios even outside of the workplace where mastering your self-talk in the realm of public speaking can serve you well.

Learning to Speak Clearly and Confidently in Public

Let's walk through the steps to using positive self-talk to create a relaxed view toward public speaking.

Step One

First you want to identify your triggers. When you think about speaking in public, what happens to you? Do you feel excited ("I can't wait to get my ideas out to the audience")? Or do you tell yourself, "I am a crummy speaker—I am bound to embarrass myself"? Think about an upcoming situation, a past event, or just imagine a circumstance where you have to speak in public. Become aware of what happens to you physically. Do you lie awake at night? Do you get sweaty palms or cold feet? Note here how you react when you think about public speaking. It can be helpful to close your eyes for a few minutes and pretend you have an upcoming speech to make. Take your time to think about how your body responds so you can capture as many details as possible about your reactions.

_____

_____

_____

Step Two

Now think about your negative self-talk. What is it about speaking in public or in important situations that bothers you?

What language do you use to talk to yourself about it? Be clear about the negative self-talk and list words and phrases you use here. Again, take your time to think about this so you can be sure you are using words that are normal for you. It's important that you can relate to whatever you write.

_____

_____

Step Three

After reading the instructions for this next step, take the time to sit quietly for a minute and close your eyes. Get a picture in your mind of the positive outcome you desire. What would you like to have happen in this situation? Would you like to see people nodding their heads and clapping enthusiastically for you? Imagine the details of this positive outcome. See yourself smiling and happy about the outcome. Sit up straight as you think about this—be confident in your body even as you imagine the scenario. Whatever you want as an outcome that's different from what has happened in the past or what you might expect, spend some time picturing it now. Feel, think, and imagine how differently you will feel once you approach public speaking with more confidence.

Step Four

Now practice your positive self-talk. Use some, or all, of the following or make up some of your own to build your confidence.

- "I am calm and confident when it comes to public speaking. I actually find I like sharing my ideas. My focus is on the audience and the message I want to deliver, not on me. I care about their experience."

- "I practice what I want to talk about so I feel confident and at ease once I speak. I prepare. I take my time in advance to ensure a positive outcome."

- "Nothing is going to happen to me that I can't deal with in this situation. I can laugh at any mistakes I might make. Even the most professional, talented public speakers make mistakes. What's the big deal? I know what I need to do and can deal with any outcome."

- "I become better and better at public speaking each time I do it. I enjoy the opportunity to improve my skills and become more talented at public speaking."

- "I can do anything that someone else can do. I see people who speak all of the time. They are not better or worse than me. I can do this just as easily as anyone else can do it. In fact, I learn from watching others and know what to do to be clear and confident and to make an impact with my speaking."

- "I focus on my audience. I focus on what they need to learn from me. I focus on making my message understandable and clear."

Repeat these self-talk options until you settle on the one or ones that fit you the best. Imagine your positive outcome and repeat some of these self-talk affirmations while you do it. Reinforce and reinforce until you can own this positive approach to public speaking.

Keep practicing the positive self-talk options until you find one that calms your mind and body. Remember that it's important to know your triggers—the way you have historically reacted to public speaking—so that when you feel triggered, you can begin the process of positive self-talk and positive visioning to see a different outcome. Use the positive self-talk as much as you need to until your mind is calm and you feel confident about your next step with public speaking and conveying the ideas that are important to you.

Working in Difficult Conditions

In too many jobs today, there is not enough time to do all that is required of you. There may have been cutbacks in the workforce. While the number of people goes down, the amount of work often does not. The people who are left are asked to take on more and more. Because they will be cut next if they can't handle the increased burden, they often don't feel they are in a position to say "no." So the work continues to pile up, and there is often no end in sight.

Or perhaps you are in a situation in which too much change is happening. There's a fire-drill environment in which you don't know what to expect from one day to the next. Perhaps it seems as if no one is in charge or that the people in charge don't know what they are doing. Perhaps you are in charge but feel incapable of managing the change process.

Or maybe you are in a job situation in which being a cultural misfit is causing you stress and angst. Your natural behavioral style is not a fit for the job you are in, and you must stretch to make it work. You might be an outgoing people-person who really wants to be in sales, but you needed a job and so find yourself working with analysis and spreadsheets. You dread going in every day and become depressed or angry, feeling your real talents are unappreciated. Possibly, you are a person who cares passionately about the environment and recycling, and yet you work for an employer that is dumping chemicals into a nearby river. Your values are in direct conflict with those of your employer, and you feel miscast working where you are.

All of these work situations can lead to an anxious mind. But it doesn't have to be that way. Positive self-talk can turn things around for you.

Hate Your Job? You Are Not Alone!

A variety of surveys have confirmed that most Americans hate their jobs. As much as 84 percent of people would leave their current employer if they thought they could. According to one study, only 5 percent of people are satisfied or happy in their job. What is causing so much unrest and distress? It can certainly be things like low pay, a bad boss, or difficult work conditions, but negative self-talk is at the root of much of it.

Positive self-talk allows you to reframe the situation. Keep the job, but talk to yourself about it differently. See if you can change the circumstances by changing the self-talk.

Reframe the Work Situation

In every job there are things that you might want to change. If you were made king or queen of your workplace tomorrow, you might have a handy list of what you would do in your new kingdom. However, it's unlikely that anyone is going to anoint you, so you have to examine your other options. One is to use self-talk to reframe the situation and look at it differently.

Of course you always reserve the right to find a new job. If you decide to do this, refer back to the earlier section within this chapter to get some ideas for positive self-talk in the job search. This self-talk exercise is about using positive tools to deal with the issues you may encounter. The art of reframing, which is what you are learning in this book with your positive self-talk, allows you to take a situation and, without changing the facts and data about it, change your impression or viewpoint of it. This means you're going to go into the same work environment tomorrow that you did today, but you'll have a different interpretation of what's happening there and different coping strategies to deal with it.

Assessing Your Current Environment

First, it's important to understand what's happening in the current workplace or job that is triggering your negative reactions. Sometimes, especially with work where you spend so much time there, you become desensitized to what's happening and begin to believe it's you, or that all workplaces are this bad. As a first step, assess the current conditions in your workplace. Identify which of the following fits your situation by circling **Y** or **N**:

There is too much change in my workplace	Y/N
No one seems to be in charge at my work or those in charge don't know what they are doing	Y/N
I am ill-fit to do the job that I do and it stresses me	Y/N
I just hate my job	Y/N
I could never get everything done even if I worked 24/7	Y/N
My employer has unrealistic expectations of me	Y/N
I dread Monday (or whatever day starts my workweek)	Y/N
I hate the culture of my firm	Y/N
This company treats people badly and has no ethics	Y/N
I would leave my job tomorrow if I could	Y/N

The Self-Talk about My Job

Now review the list above. For which statements did you circle Y? What negative aspects of the job or your work situation stood out for you? Do you have a generalized feeling of hating everything, or are you upset about specific things that are happening at your job?

Next, write your negative self-talk associated with your job. Review the list or write about other things that you haven't identified here. Be as detailed as you can about examples of your negative self-talk. What do you think about your job, or your workplace environment? How do you feel about it? What words do you use to talk to yourself about your job?

_____

_____

Change the Frame

You may have many coworkers or colleagues who agree with you. The talk about the bad situation at work might be so prevalent that everyone has come to accept it as fact. Some things may even *be* factual. Perhaps your employer really is dumping those chemicals into the water; clearly you don't want to view this action positively. The self-talk you change here is not about giving your boss or the company you work for a pass on bad behavior. If your employer is engaged in unethical (or even illegal) behavior, you may want to leave the job or thoughtfully confront someone about these issues. But if what's happened is that you have developed a bad attitude about your work, this next section will be very helpful for you.

The Step-by-Step Process

You have circled some thoughts you have about your workplace. Take a moment to read these again and become aware of how thinking about them triggers you. Do you become depressed? Do you start to think "How did I wind up in this situation?" or "There is no way out"? Notice what reactions you have to thinking about your work. Capture any thoughts now. If you can write the negative self-talk you use, do that now too.

_____

_____

_____

Step One
Imagine how you would like to feel about your job. Do you want to go into the office or workplace every day feeling upbeat and enthusiastic? Create a picture of how you'd like to approach work. Do you care if it is fulfilling? Do you think that you can manage whatever comes your way? That you have good relationships with others even through turbulence? What do you strive toward, and what would success look like to you?

_____

_____

_____

Step Two

Now take a minute to sit quietly and imagine what it is like to get up in the morning and love what you do for a living. Imagine you have the same attitude going to work as you would if you were going out on a weekend to do something you love. Take those same feelings that you have when you are excited and enthusiastic about something, or even just feeling positive and energized, and transfer them to your thoughts about going into work. It can be helpful to close your eyes and picture the positive feelings in any way you can. However, if you don't want to do this, that's fine. Not everyone "sees" pictures in their minds. Just imagine good feelings, a happy attitude toward work, and confidence in dealing with whatever comes your way in the workplace.

Step Three

Now, practice positive self-talk. Read the following phrases and see which ones most fit you and your situation or which ones you can most relate to and seem the most "real" to you.

- "My job is just a place I go to make my living. I can choose to think of it as a temporary stop, and therefore feel detached whenever I want to escape from what's happening there."

- "I can deal confidently and completely with anything that comes my way in the workplace. After all, it's just work."

- "Even though my work is demanding and important, I am able to step back, think about what I need to do, and then approach my work thoughtfully and confidently. I am in control of my actions and reactions."

- "My attitude makes all of the difference in my workplace. I choose a positive attitude every day. I choose an attitude of wanting to learn. I think of work as 'paid learning.'"

- "All workplaces have issues. Mine are no worse than anyone else's. I choose to look at things at work objectively and calmly."

- "I believe in myself. I believe in my abilities. I believe I can make a difference at my workplace no matter how small. I look for ways to make a difference every day."

- "Attitude is everything. I surround myself with positive people at work. I focus on what's good. I look for the silver lining every day."

Step Four

Now put this all together. Imagine you are happy in your work. You are confident. You feel good about what you do—whether it is making hamburgers at a fast-food restaurant, investing millions of dollars in the stock market, or laying brick for a new apartment building. It doesn't matter what the work is; you see yourself approaching work with confidence, with anticipation of positive things that might happen, and with an attitude of openness and learning. You can choose the self-talk that will make these pictures real for you. Review the self-talk above and repeat the words over and over again. Let them sink in. The way you get up in the morning and decide to face the workday will have everything to do with what you encounter there. Even if things go "wrong" (the boss gives you more work or yells at you; the computer crashes; or the truck you need isn't working), your positive self-talk can guide you through the day to deal with it all more effectively and with more confidence.

Choosing to have a different attitude toward work and modifying your self-talk about it is in your hands. If you, like most people, spend the majority of your time at your workplace, you may want to have a better attitude toward it and a more fulfilling experience of it. By using positive self-talk toward work, you gain a new perspective and calm your anxious mind.

CHAPTER 7

Dealing with Life Changes, Creating Life Changes

Many people want to make life changes—be they small or large. No matter what is currently happening in your life, whether you're doing what you love or struggling to find a path that fits you, setting and achieving personal goals is an essential part of your growth as a person. But making a coveted change happen can be difficult. All too often you get in your own way. Statistics show that as many as half the people who set a new year's resolution abandon it by the sixth month of the new year. You probably want to effect some sort of change—most people do—but learning how to set an objective, move toward it, and eventually meet the goal is challenging for many. For some people, setting the goal in the first place is the most challenging part of the process. You just can't even find the time, space, or motivation to sit down and figure out what you really want. You've heard that you should take the time to write goals down or spend time thinking about what you really want and why you want it. But you just haven't been able to get motivated or focused enough to do even this first step. Your goal remains vague and undefined.

Or maybe you set the goal, but then find yourself fizzling out before you can even see moderate changes start to happen. You buy exercise equipment and new workout clothes, but after the first week, you never use them again. You write a new resume and apply for jobs, but after the first three "nos," you abandon the job search entirely. You start out with good intentions, and you may even take some steps to move you closer to where you eventually want to be, but something happens along the way and takes you off your track. Oftentimes what stops you from setting the goal, or interrupts your process, is the negative self-talk. It can find all of the reasons why the path you are on isn't going to lead anywhere. It can deter you and make you wonder why you ever thought you could head in a new direction in the first place. Remember that negative self-talk is very practiced within you for telling you what you can't do. Because of this, in order to make any lasting life change, you have to overcome your own personal challenges if you're going to get to your desired goal.

The Power of (Bad) Habits

Making a change is particularly hard for many people because human beings are creatures of habit. People often prefer the tried-and-true to the unknown. Somehow that adage "the devil we know is better than the one we don't" has become ingrained in cultural thinking.

Many times change is forced upon you, and it may not be something you want. However, life hands us new challenges all of the time. The only constant in life *is* change, so if you aren't experiencing something now, you likely will be sometime soon.

Of course, the change could be for the better. Your reaction to it dictates whether navigating it is easy or difficult for you. What you may not realize is that the self-talk about change and the choices you make about it will impact much of the eventual result. When going through a change, especially one that is thrust upon you, it's often hard to manage self-talk. You feel a "victim" or helpless in the face of the change. You may not even recognize the self-talk that accompanies every step you take along the way.

The first step is awareness. Think about whether you want to take charge of an upcoming change. If something is happening and you'd prefer to have a different experience as you go through it, self-talk can be very powerful. Similarly if you want to effect a change you've been hoping to make, self-talk can provide support and confidence as you move forward.

Self-Talk—with All the Wrong Words

The important thing to remember is that self-talk can make all the difference one way or the other. You may think about the change you want to make one moment and be motivated to action, and then find yourself on the couch glued to the television the next moment. How does that happen? Your self-talk kicked in and told you not to bother with the goal. You were feeling down and disconsolate about the future and wanted to give up. But maybe the next day, everything seemed brighter and you got back on track. Why? Your positive self-talk reenergized you.

Observe how this might be happening to you, where you have good intentions one moment but then an opposite negative experience the next. When you are watchful about it, you may see that it occurs multiple times throughout the day. For example, as discussed earlier, in a new year or at a birthday many people make resolutions. You might know what you want to accomplish—lose some weight, learn a language, take a much-desired trip—and so you set the goal for the year.

What happens next? For many people, the self-talk that has defeated you before rears its ugly head again. "I have never been able to take that trip to Paris. It's so expensive. What made me think this year would be different?" You may have wanted to be healthier this year so you make the commitment to eat well, exercise more, and lose the weight. And yet you find yourself sitting at the kitchen table eating a box of cookies with negative self-talk as your company saying, "This weight has been on since I had my last child, seventeen years ago. I'm older. It's never going to leave me. I may as well just have another cookie. Tomorrow is another day."

This sort of thing happens to everyone. Negative self-talk continues to bring you back to your failures. It wants to keep you stuck in the groove you have been in. This is why making a coveted change can be hard—your self-talk doesn't set you up for success.

Self-Talk as the Solution

If you are committed to making a change and ready to take charge of this aspect of your life, let's look at how self-talk can be managed and used to help you navigate an undesired change, or move in a confident direction toward a desired one. In fact, the most important change you will make is to take charge of your self-talk. Why continue to be dragged down by this negativity when you can change the story you tell yourself to something more positive, more beneficial, that gives you the energy and drive to move forward?

First, tell that inner voice that you aren't listening to negativity anymore. The only voices you want to listen to are the ones guiding you and telling you where you need to go and what's good for you. You can select what you will focus on and what you will say to yourself. You can choose to listen only to those voices that tell you healthy, positive things that propel you forward. Uninvite those negative naysayers and invite in the voices who say "I am moving forward. I am taking the right steps every day toward my goals. I am energized and enthused about where I am going next!"

Step One

You want to know where you are going. What's the goal you desire? First, identify, in writing, what you'd like to accomplish or what a new you would look like or be experiencing. Look at what's happening now. Identify specifically what you'd like to change.

Catch yourself and review your thoughts right now. In this moment. Did you think, *This never works for me! In fact, I hate writing things down.* Or did you think, *I am finally going to focus on this!* All day long we have a conversation with ourselves without even knowing we are doing it.

Before you go any further, deliberately suspend your thinking. How do you do this? By clearing your mind of any thoughts—good or bad. It means not mentally running ahead and thinking about what's next or ruminating over what is happening right now. Let any thoughts you have flow through, as if your mind is a sieve, leaving you open and receptive. Read the words written here but don't dwell too long on them. Don't judge anything or talk to yourself about it. If you find yourself talking, or reacting, review what you learned in Chapter 3 about recognition. Much of the practice to turn negative self-talk into positive self-talk is to recognize, choose to suspend judgment, and then be deliberate about what you want your mind to focus on. Now proceed with the assessment.

Fill in the following in as much detail as you can about the change you want to make.

1. If I could change anything in my life, I would change:

    _____

2. If I did what I want to do, success would look like this to me:

    _____

Now sit quietly. If you want to, close your eyes. Take a moment to picture in your mind what this goal or changed state looks like to you. How do you feel about it? What do you think about once you've reached this changed state? What's happening there? What emotions do you associate with it? If you can, write down some qualitative and quantitative things that will happen once you get to this new state.

Step Two

Now let's explore your self-talk around goal setting and change management. You have identified your goal. You have put it in writing and can vision it somehow for your future. It's time to assess what your self-talk says about your ability to meet this goal and be successful.

To do this exercise, be sure you are in a place with no distractions. You need some time to focus, so don't start this when you've got errands to run or someone might ring your doorbell or call your phone. As you think about this goal and imagine the change you want to make, list the following ideas.

1. My worries about making this change include:

    _____

2. My biggest fear about this change is:

    _____

3. The words I use to describe my fear/worry/concern about this change include:

    _____

Acknowledge that these are your obstacles. You want to own them but then release them. Look at the list of things you have written and say to yourself, "I used to worry about these things. My attitude is shifting, and I have a different belief system now. My self-talk about making a desired change is positive and energizing to me."

Next, identify specifically why you can make this change happen and why it will work for you. If the change is important to you, there are reasons you believe you *can* do it, and you *want* to do it.

1. I'm confident I can make this change because:

    _____

    _____

2. I have done similar things in the past like:

_____

_____

3. This is an important change for me to make because:

_____

_____

Now look at both lists. Circle those words that resonate with you—those that are negative and those that are positive. Choose the words that trigger you the most to the point that you have a visceral reaction to them. Think about what these words mean to you. What associations come to you from these words? Are they formed by good or bad past experiences? Think about why they have a weight with you. Write any thoughts here about those words.

My negative triggers:

_____

My positive triggers:

_____

You especially want to take note of those negative triggers. Those words may creep in at some point to tell you why this isn't going to work and persuade you that you needn't even bother trying. From now on, you will be attuned to them. Every time you hear one, you must make a conscious decision to reject it. If negative self-talk starts to creep in, you can say, for example, "I used to worry that I did not have self-confidence, but my belief system has changed. Now I know I am confident enough to make arrangements to travel to Paris on my own." Use whatever words fit your situation. Keep noticing the negative words and ideas and replacing them with your positive words. Refer back to your lists as often as necessary to ensure you are pulling in words and themes that are already triggers for you.

Step Three

Now it is time to examine what choices you have to help you manage this change or get to this desired goal. Get very practical here. What can you do to obviate your worries? What tools or resources might you have that will help you on your journey? You will want to use positive self-talk to tell yourself you are resourceful, you are able to find solutions, and you can figure out the necessary steps you need. You *can* manage this!

Make a list:

1. What I can do to overcome my concerns:

    _____

    _____

2. The tools/resources I possess:

    _____

    _____

Stopping Negativity in Its Tracks

Part of the power of positive self-talk is having something to offset a negative thought or negative reaction. As you move along the path of change, a worry will pop into your mind. "I can't do this. It's too hard." Have your list in front of you. What can you do to overcome a worry? What tools do you possess? Use these lists as your guideposts. Keep them close by so you can grab them whenever you need them. When the negative self-talk comes in (and it will come in, so be prepared!), you have offsetting ideas to deal with it.

CASE STUDY

Let's consider Jocelyn, a single mother, forty-six years old with two children. Lately she's started to feel out of breath and out of shape. So on her last birthday she told herself, "I'm going to lose weight. I'm going to go to the gym regularly, eat healthy food, and find a physically and mentally challenging hobby."

It's two months later, and she's sitting at the kitchen table, feeling gloomy and out of sorts. In front of her is a box of cookies, most of them gone. What happened?

Negative self-talk, that's what. Jocelyn was all set to make a big change in her lifestyle, and then she began to tell herself, "This weight has been on since I had my last child, seventeen years ago. I'm older. It's never going to leave me. I may as well just have another cookie. Tomorrow is another day."

Jocelyn has let herself be guided by her negative self-talk. But the change in her life is too important for her to put it off any longer. Instead, she resolves to tell that inner voice that she's not listening to negativity anymore. Instead, she realizes that she can proactively select what she will focus on and what she will say to herself. She will listen only to those voices that tell her healthy, positive things that propel her forward. She says to herself, "I am moving forward. I am taking the right steps every day toward my goals. I am energized and enthused about where I am going next!"

Now Jocelyn sets her goal. She thinks, *I want to be twenty-five pounds lighter. I also want to be fitter. I want to go up a flight of stairs without puffing. And I want to look good in a nice dress. I want to be able to buy pretty clothes, not shapeless ones that hide my figure. And I want people to notice me and think about how great I look.*

Of course, one part of her mind says, "This never works for me! These are impossible goals." But the stronger voice, the one Jocelyn chooses to listen to, says, "I am finally going to focus on this! My health is important, and I'm going to be happier when I lose this weight and have a healthy lifestyle."

Jocelyn reviews her list to see what choices she has and how positive self-talk can help her.

In the past when she was tired or depressed, she sat down in her kitchen and ate—usually something unhealthy. Now she's going to make a different choice. She's going to leave the kitchen and take a walk. When she's upset about something or feeling down, she puts on earphones, listens to upbeat music, walks out the door to get exercise, and reminds herself about her weight loss goal.

As she does so, she tells herself, "This is good for me. I'm energized. I can feel the calories burning away. I can feel my heart and my other muscles working, toning, making me stronger."

Jocelyn has started to move from a defeated stance, to a more positive, "What can I do next?" approach. Each time she feels like giving in, she thinks about the options she has available. She keeps a list of them on her refrigerator door so she can refer to them easily.

After a couple of days of thinking (and exercising), Jocelyn's list looks like this:

What I can do to overcome my concerns:

- Every time I feel compelled to eat food that isn't good for me, I take a walk instead.
- I can remove fattening food from my cupboards.
- I can be a more deliberate shopper and choose snacks and food that are healthy for me.
- I can find a buddy to exercise with.

The tools/resources I possess:

- The power of my mind—I can say more positive things like: "Weight loss is a process. Every day I take one step closer to my goal." Or, "I make good decisions when it comes to food choices."
- Access to nutritional websites (Jocelyn lists some URLs here for easy convenience)

The items on the list serve as Jocelyn's guideposts, showing her the path to her goal, giving her comfort, and reminding her she can do it. She's eliminated those negative voices by replacing them with positive, more powerful options.

Finding Your Bliss

Next, let's look at another aspect of life change and then review how you can take charge of your self-talk to break through once and for all. Let's examine dealing with life disappointments, uncovering roadblocks, and identifying your bliss.

It seems for many people life is a series of one disappointment after another. Have you ever said to yourself, "If I didn't have bad luck, I'd have no luck at all"? You might set out with positive intention and be upbeat and excited about what's next, but then find yourself dealing with the same setback over and over. For some people this can occur when they are moving from job to job, never finding that right fit for them. For others, it manifests as yo-yo dieting, watching that weight go up and down from month to month. Some people struggle to find the love of their life only to realize that person wasn't the right one after all. Many people, faced with this, wonder "What's wrong with me?" or blame the world for their trouble.

If you don't feel the joie de vivre in your life, it's time to use the power of self-talk to get off the sidelines and start enjoying your bliss in life. Let's look at steps you can take to find your personal bliss: the place where you feel content, and happy with your life. It is attainable, but only by using positive self-talk and focusing on what's working.

Step One

What is your bliss? How would you define it? What would make you get up in the morning and feel like singing with the birds? Even if you have set your goals and are moving confidently in the direction of your dreams, you want to know what your bliss looks like. Bliss is defined as the place where you feel content, peaceful, and have a sense of joy. It is the difference between moving away from something and moving toward something. As a first step, you want to identify what you want to move toward. What draws you? Be clear about what you really care about, and where you want to be. Defining your "bliss" can be hard. Most people know what they don't want, but don't take the time to think about what they do want. Take the time to picture your bliss—define it.

_____

_____

_____

Now, turn to the disappointment(s) you may have suffered and where your quest for bliss has historically gone awry. What happened? Write this here:

1. I thought I was going to achieve/accomplish/get this:

   _____

   _____

2. Instead I got this:

   _____

   _____

Review the steps you took to get where you thought would be good for you. Was there a certain point at which the process started to go awry? Can you diagnose where you went off track? What self-talk accompanied the process?

Think about what you believed about your goal:

1. I felt confident I was doing the right thing because:

   _____

   _____

2. I believe this about my journey:

   _____

   _____

It's important to uncover your beliefs about yourself and about life. Sometimes these are self-limiting thoughts and behaviors that stop us before we even start a new journey. Don't hesitate to look at these. It's important to bring them to the surface and examine them. Don't reject them or say, "I shouldn't think this way." Instead bring them up so you can formally uninvite them!

Step Two

Set the objective differently this time. Instead of finding the love of your life, the job you desire, or the lifestyle you want, look at the big picture. What makes you happy? Why do you desire certain things? What really matters to you?

Let's take a love interest. Some people might say, "I just want to meet someone. I am tired of being alone." This is a recipe for trouble. If you settle for someone—anyone—it won't be long before you find out that this person is not what you wanted after all. That provides an opening for your negative self-talk. Little voices start to whisper that you just can't attract a good mate.

It's better to be clear from the start about what you want. What qualities in a loved one really matter to you? What do you want him to care about? What values do you want her to have? What do you want to do together? What questions do you want to ask her? What do you want your parents to think when they meet him? Paint a picture that is clear and specific and that takes into account problems and disappointments from your past. Write your thoughts about how you would like it to look here.

_____

_____

_____

Now choose positive self-talk to help guide you and keep you on track. Review the list here, or make up a few statements of your own.

- "I move with intention toward my dreams."
- "I am able to reach a blissful place in my life."
- "I deserve to be happy. I move toward happiness every day."
- "I am careful about my choices. I do things that benefit me and move me closer to my bliss."
- "I can choose to be happy now."
- "Happiness is a state of mind. My state of mind is focused on happiness."

Step Three

Now put it all together. First, be sure to post your desired outcome where you can view it often. Cut out pictures of your bliss. Have a screen saver on your computer or tablet that reminds you of what you hope to achieve when you reach your own personal nirvana. Remember that your bliss could come from mastering positive self-talk and learning to take life more positively overall, without really changing anything except your mindset and responses to life.

Spend a minimum of fifteen minutes three times a day sitting quietly and saying your positive self-talk statements. If you can find a quiet spot and close your eyes, try to relax and focus your mind on what you do want. Focus on where you want to be and the good feelings and thoughts you will have once you get there. Imagine yourself in a blissful state, feeling good about life and good about where you are.

Keep the positive self-talk going at all times. Carry the affirmations with you to remind yourself when you need them. When you feel yourself in danger of giving in to negative self-talk, make a conscious choice to stop. Become aware of the language you use that defeats you.

Sometimes it can be useful to have a physical interruption to negative self-talk. When you recognize that those bad voices have taken over, shake your body as if you were literally shaking off the negativity and allowing yourself to open to more positive options. You can also jump up and down to release the negative self-talk. Imagine that you are a duck and you are covered with water. Shake your feathers and your tail to get the water off. It doesn't matter if you're sitting down or standing up. Shake, shake, shake until you feel the negativity releasing. Then, very importantly, replace it with the positive self-talk suggestions you have worked on.

Whatever you do, do something physical to send a message to your mind from your body, because the negative cycle has to be broken.

Remember that, to take on a new habit, you may have to spend a minimum of twenty-one days consistently practicing it. Especially when it comes to finding your bliss, it won't change overnight. You will want to continue to practice and reinforce your new behaviors every chance you get in order to work toward the blissful state you desire.

CHAPTER 8

Managing Stressful Situations

For many people experiencing stress seems as natural as eating or sleeping. In fact, overeating, sleepless nights, and aches and pains are often a direct result of stress. While some stress is innate—think about the fight-or-flight response all human beings possess—a lot of the stress you experience zaps your energy and makes you less effective. If you were experiencing appropriate stress levels, you would still have energy for other things. Unfortunately, as a result of unwanted stress, you may be burning through your energy, feeling as drained as a dishrag most of the time. When difficult situations arise, you cannot cope because you are exhausted and depleted.

The issue of self-talk related to stress is a bit like the chicken and the egg. Which comes first? Does your negative self-talk raise your anxiety and resulting stress levels, or does the existence of stress in your life lead to negative self-talk and self-flagellation? While it can be interesting to ponder, it's not important to solve this problem—we know they both feed on one another. What *is* important is to figure out what's triggering the stress. That's the place where negative self-talk starts in and leads you down a negative path, resulting in more and more stress.

You know by now that your negative self-talk hurts the situation. It clouds your view and limits your options. You also know that once you identify your triggers, you can see when negative self-talk starts, stop it in its tracks, turn it into positive self-talk, and give yourself more options for managing stress.

Watching It Unfold

Think about a situation that causes you some anxiety. You know the feeling—you begin to get nervous. Your palms might get sweaty. Your breathing becomes shallow and rapid. You may have a nervous tic, or perhaps you bite your fingernails. You may talk too fast or be unable to speak coherently. You may begin to imagine terrible things happening. Your pulse quickens and your throat tightens even though nothing appears to be wrong.

This is how stress works. You may never say to yourself, "I'm stressed." You may not notice how stress builds over time and takes more and more of your energy away. You just realize at some point that you feel awful. The headaches take a toll; you pop too many stomach acid pills; and you can't fall asleep at night no matter what you try.

Say "Hello!" to Your Negative Self-Talk

Negative self-talk loves stress. It loves to feed on stressful situations and use them to tell you why your life is a mess. It's a curious dynamic. You might think your negative self-talk gives you ideas for getting out of the stress, that it is a companion to help you analyze what's going on. But in reality the negative self-talk feeds on your stressful state, and your stressful state increases with the negative self-talk. You lose your ability to deal effectively with life.

It's important to notice where negative self-talk kicks in during times of stress so that you can catch it and turn your attention to more positive self-talk. Let's look at a number of situations that people deal with related to stress.

Acting Out Stress

In many panic attacks, stress manifests in a physical form. You feel a crushing weight on your chest as if you are having a heart attack. You may perspire or breathe in an exaggerated fashion. You may develop tics, tap your fingers rapidly, or constantly cross and uncross your legs. Whichever of these experiences you may relate to, they have one thing in common—your body gets involved. You have a physical reaction or sensation in response to the stress that's driving you. If you were able to step outside your body, for example, you could see the nervous tic. You could see yourself grab your chest as you try to alleviate the crushing weight you feel.

The good news is that you can begin to see your patterns. You can begin to diagnose how you and your body react to the stressful state.

Think about your stressful reactions. What happens to you, physically, when you get so stressed or so panicked that you are unable to function? Write it down. For example, you might write, "I have random panic attacks when I am driving on the highway late at night. I start to perspire and hyperventilate. I have to open the window and let air in because I become overheated and have a hard time focusing on driving."

Write anything you are aware of here:

_____

_____

If you aren't sure how you react, carry a small notebook or type notes on your smartphone or some other device. When you recognize a physical reaction coming on, note what happens. How do you react? What feelings do you have? What physical reaction occurs? Note these as they happen and look for patterns. Don't diagnose the "why"; just observe what happens so you can become more familiar with your own patterns.

Recognizing the Signs

It's hard to "step outside" yourself and pull back once you are fully in the grip of the stressful state. For this reason, you should work on recognizing the onset of the physical symptoms. You want to know when the pressure is beginning to mount. You want to realize that your stress levels are escalating so you can make different choices—but in order to realize it, you must recognize how it manifests within you.

There is no one-size-fits-all approach. You must be able to diagnose or assess how situations impact you. Only when you are able to see what happens to you can you decide to make different choices and bring positive self-talk in to help you.

Once you have recognized the physical reactions, back up to what triggers them. You have learned a lot about triggers in this book, and you should continue to question your triggers that start to pull you down the proverbial rabbit hole and into increasingly negative self-talk. Think about the situations that stress you. What happens right before you start to have the physical reactions? Do you think about something? Do you experience something? Does something go wrong? Or are they simply random? You can't really pinpoint what starts the cycle and allows your negative responses to come upon you? There are no right or wrong answers here. It's what you experience. Note anything you are aware of here:

_____

_____

Holding Your Negative Reactions Accountable

Next, think about these negative reactions as "visitors." The physical reactions you have are temporary residents in your body, but they don't really belong to you. The situations may be real, but the stressful automatic responses are not. These are learned behaviors. They are reactions you have practiced and you have begun to wear as your own, but you can choose at any time to uninvite them and make a different choice. Positive self-talk can help you do this.

When it comes to stress, here are some of the positive self-talk options you have available to you. You will want to call upon these when you know you are entering into a stressful situation or when your body reminds you that a negative visitor has taken up residence there.

Step One

Review this list and circle those positive self-talk statements that have meaning to you. As you read each line, which ones induce peace for you? Which ones resonate with you and seem to calm you? Which ones can you just relate to?

- "This too shall pass. This is a point in time; it isn't my whole life."
- "I am bigger than any situation I face. I was made to deal with my life and everything that comes to me."

- "I am calm. I am confident. I control my own reactions."
- "Getting uptight doesn't help me. It brings me down. I make different choices now."
- "I have the choice to take deep breaths. Slowly breathing in, slowly breathing out. Each breath out removes the toxin from my body, and each breath in replaces it with calming, healing comfort."
- "Every time I give in to anxiety and stress, I lose my edge. I keep my edge and am in control."
- "I go into my personal zone. I am strong. I am in charge of my life and my reactions."
- "The negative feelings that visit me don't belong to me. I uninvite them. I invite in only positive, healthy reactions. My body is clear; my mind is clear; and I feel good."

Step Two

As you review this list of positive self-talk options, circle the ones that resonate with you. If none seem to fit, write a variation of any of them that feels more aligned with you. You will want to practice these until they become mantras for you. In other cases within this book, you have looked at some specific situations for which you might be able to prepare or have a plan in advance. In the case of panic attacks, generalized anxiety disorder, OCD, or the like, you may not know when the stress will come upon you. You could be walking down the street on a beautiful sunny day, and all of a sudden the panic attack jumps you from behind. Because of this, it's important to develop a mantra. It's important to have some positive self-talk standing at the ready, waiting for you to call upon it.

Work in ways throughout your day to practice these mantras so you are in a position to call upon them at any point in time. Because you will need to close your eyes, read these instructions through a couple of times so you know what to do. When you are ready, begin this exercise. This one requires an ongoing commitment. Because you don't know when you will need it, you must practice the "waiting" and preparing every day.

Step Three

Find a quiet place to sit down for a few minutes each day. Do this at least three or four times per day for at least three to five minutes at a time. Three times take a deep breath in and picture clean, cleansing air filling your lungs and your body. When you exhale, picture all stress, all negativity, and all concern leaving your body. Breathe this way until you actually feel your body getting calmer and more peaceful.

When you are ready, and your breathing is deep and calming, close your eyes. Sit for a few minutes and focus on your breath. Imagine that you can see the air as it fills your lungs and as it leaves when you exhale. Focus only on the breath; if thoughts or words come into your mind, gently push them away. Imagine there is a man with a broom inside your head. He gently sweeps away any thoughts that want to visit. If you have a phobia toward brooms—or men—imagine another image like this that works for you.

As you sit quietly, repeat your mantra to yourself over and over. You may say it quietly under your breath as a whisper, or you may say it only in your head without speaking out loud at all. As best you can, picture the words as you say them. Some people like to add a musical tone to the words, and some like to chant them. Some like to add modulation or a somber tone. Whatever helps you to grab these words, makes them stick, and gives them impact is right for you.

Be sure to spend the entire three to five minutes with this mantra. Feel your body at peace. Think about how the deep breathing calms you. Don't rush through this. Even with all you have to do, nine to twelve minutes out of your day isn't going to put you farther behind. Instead you may find once you finish the exercise that you are clearer and more energized to finish what you have to do.

It's critically important to do this exercise every single day. You want to be prepared for the stressors when they come visit. You must have a plan to take a different path of action.

CASE STUDY

What does this look like in action? Let's meet Leonard. He's twenty-nine years old and works in a top financial firm in New York, where daily he juggles millions of dollars. His job is consuming, and as a result of it he's under constant stress. Lately it's become debilitating to the point that he's made some costly mistakes and drawn the unwelcome attention of his supervisors.

Increasingly, Leonard is subject to panic attacks. He wakes in the middle of the night, feeling something massive pressing down on his chest. The sheets are drenched in sweat; his forehead is clammy; and his throat is dry. His heart is racing, but according to his physician he's not had a heart attack. Rather, he's under extreme stress.

A part of Leonard's brain is constantly nagging him: "You're not that good at what you're doing. Suppose you make a huge mistake? Suppose your clients lose their entire investment? Suppose you lose your job and word goes around the street that you're unreliable? You could lose everything: the great Manhattan apartment, the cool car, the Rolex watch." This is negative self-talk feeding all of Leonard's doubts and insecurities.

But now he knows he's got to break the cycle. He sits down in his kitchen and jots down on a pad a series of positive statements about himself.

- "I'm good at my job. That's why I'm one of the youngest traders in the firm."
- "Every day I make money for my clients by using my skills and knowledge."
- "I have a great life—and with hard work and perseverance, I can keep it great."

He goes to the living room, his favorite room in the apartment. With some music playing very quietly in the background, he draws the curtains so the room is in partial darkness. Then he sits in a chair, comfortable and calm, breathing in and out, imagining all his stress and concerns flowing away from his body.

Softly he says his three mantras, repeating them over and over for five minutes. At the end, he spends another minute breathing calmly, enjoying the silence.

Repeating this routine at the beginning and end of every day, Leonard starts to find that the symptoms of his panic attacks are easing. His positive self-talk is turning around his life. He is clearer and more focused at his job, and as a result he is making better decisions. His boss now sees him as more confident and in control.

Practice Makes Perfect

You may want to write your positive self-talk on a card that you carry with you. Or you may want to post several notes around to remind you of your mantra. The more you access it, the easier it will be to call upon it when you need to. The next important step is to bring it into the picture when the physical reaction to stress starts to visit you.

Become aware of the situations that stress you out. If you know you tend to have the panic attack while driving at night, practice your positive self-talk for a few minutes before you go out. If you have OCD and know that you are prone to revisit your home several times to assure yourself that everything is as it should be, practice the sayings each time you are ready to leave. In order to make positive self-talk work for you, you must assess where you need it and prepare.

Preparing for Stressful Life Situations

We talked earlier about a generalized stress reaction. It can happen anywhere at any time without much notice. Of course, sometimes you'll know something potentially bad is going to happen. Often you hope for the best but expect the worst. Your negative self-talk helps ratchet up your anxiety in these situations. In fact, the outcome can be positive or negative, but your negative self-talk will always assure you that the worst is waiting for you around the corner.

The truth is that there are difficult situations in life. There is sadness and pain. People we love die. People get sick and suffer. People lose jobs and spouses. Positive self-talk doesn't delude you into thinking that life isn't life. You won't pretend that everything is beautiful when it isn't. What positive self-talk can do is help you get through these difficult or sad situations with a different attitude. It can help focus your attention, clarify your ideas, and give you energy to complete whatever tasks lie ahead.

Think about someone you know who was terminally ill but maintained a positive attitude. That person didn't believe the positive attitude would "save" him, but he wanted to enjoy whatever time he had left. Think about people who have been through a divorce but chose to remain friends even just for the sake of their kids. Think about someone who might have been fired from a job, unable to pay her bills, but still volunteered at a homeless shelter. There are people who suffer through very difficult and painful situations in life and seem to come out fine. One man I knew well was put in prison for something he didn't do. He kept a positive attitude, refused to look at those years as lost, and instead turned that experience into something positive that others have learned from. If negative self-talk is "right," then why doesn't everyone crumple under the weight of difficulty? Because the self-talk you choose often dictates your ability to be resilient, to find solutions, and to focus on the silver lining.

Stop the Pain!

Most people who are experiencing a difficult time simply want it to be over. "I can't wait until my divorce is final." "I wish they would just give me the pink slip and be done with it. The waiting is killing me." "I will be so happy when this year ends!"

Instead of plowing through these negative situations, let's look at ways you can use them to practice your positive self-talk and potentially adopt a new attitude or approach to dealing with what befalls you.

Think about an upcoming event that is causing you stress, or one you are going through now. Write down what might happen, and what you are expecting. So, for example, you might write: "My company is in financial trouble. Layoffs have been happening all around me. I have heard through the grapevine that my unit is next. It's just a matter of time before I get my pink slip."

_____

_____

_____

_____

Now—this is important—write about what you expect will happen to you from this situation. Often people tell themselves a story about how this incident will destroy them. For example, you might write: "If I lose my job, I can't send my kids to college. I can't even pay the mortgage on my house. There are no jobs out there. I'm doomed to live eating cat food—and what will I feed my cats? We will all starve."

_____

_____

_____

_____

Be sure to take some time to write this out. Much of what you will write is actually the negative self-talk that visits you about this situation. These are the beliefs you now hold about how this upcoming situation will affect your life. You might write these outcomes and feel confident they are going to happen, but really—at this moment—you are writing a play. It's true that your company might be going through layoffs and you might be next, but what happens after that is all conjecture fueled by your negative self-talk.

Next, identify your resources. Identify those attributes, skills, support systems, intellectual abilities, and strengths you possess that could help you deal more effectively with the upcoming situation. For example, you might write: "I am a very skilled employee. I offer a lot of value to my employer because no one else knows how to run the system that I do." Or, "I have been through hard times before. I always manage to pick myself up, dust myself off, and start all over again!"

_____

_____

_____

_____

The next part of this exercise is critically important because it's going to ask you to question beliefs you likely hold very dear. For example, you may truly believe that the self-talk you are using about the upcoming event *is* true. You *will* be eating cat food. You won't ever get another job. You are doomed. What you need to do next is shine a strong light on those beliefs and look at them closely. They are only beliefs at this point. They are not facts.

The truth is that every situation has many possible outcomes. Some outcomes you might prefer more than others, but there are many ways your life could turn out. Until the final act, you don't really know what is coming around the corner.

Most situations have both a positive and negative aspect. Yes, it's hard if the love of your life leaves you for another person, but it's also liberating that you no longer live with someone who was lying to you. Yes, going to jail for a crime you did not commit is a terrible tragedy, but taking those experiences, writing about them, and working to change a broken system is a positive outcome. Most causes and movements are started because someone experiences something so awful that they don't want anyone else to have to go through it. In other words, it's virtually always possible to change a negative outcome to a positive one.

Now you might be saying, "She has rose-colored glasses on. She is trying to paint a happy picture where one doesn't belong."

This is why it's critical to loosen your long-held beliefs just a little bit. If you won't consider that there could be another way to look at the stressful situation, then there isn't a point in completing this exercise. If you want to have more power, more options, and more strength in dealing with stress, you have to let go of the belief that you "know" what is right and what is wrong and that you "know" what will happen next.

Write two scenarios about the situation you are facing. In them, develop a story of two possible positive outcomes. This may take some creative writing on your part, but force yourself to think about two ways the situation *could* go that might have some positive attributes.

For example, let's go back to the situation at work where you expect the pink slip. Two possible outcomes could include:

"I have been doing such a good job here and am very valued. They can't lay off everyone so even though it pains me to see my coworkers in pain and losing their jobs, I am going to be here for a long time to come. I will adopt a positive attitude and keep upbeat throughout the process." Or alternatively, you could think:

"I might lose my job, but the truth is I have hated it here. I really want to do something else, but I have been too scared to leave. When I get the pink slip, it will motivate me to follow my dreams. It might be hard financially, but I will find a way to make it work. There is always a solution if I look hard enough."

_____

_____

_____

_____

The point of creating these two options is to show you that there isn't only one foregone conclusion about how the stressful life situation will end. Through negative self-talk, you tell yourself a story—you write the plot line and "know" how everything will turn out. This is why your stress level continues to rise. There doesn't seem to be another option. By forcing yourself to write about other options, you can see that there *are* other possible outcomes. In times of trouble, if your self-talk is only focused on how horrible everything is, you can't allow yourself the chance to recharge your batteries or find any positive outcomes.

In the midst of dealing with anything, you can use positive self-talk to calm yourself and find ways to focus on something other than the worry or sadness brought on by the situation. There are cases even when a close friend or relative is dying of a terminal disease in which people still find joy in small ways— possibly by caring for the person. Sometimes when you're with someone who is dying, old wounds are healed or words are spoken that haven't been said before. Sometimes both of you are able to let go of past hurts or difficulties.

It's not to say that the solution to stress is simply to look on the bright side—it's not. You have to be realistic and objective about whatever difficulties are facing you. And I'm not saying that there aren't difficult emotions you will have to deal with as you go through challenging life experiences. But becoming drained and stressed weakens your resources. You need to be strong and clear-headed. You always have an opportunity to use your self-talk to direct the situation and your reaction to it. Your self-talk can either defeat you early on or give you the power to stay open and curious about what can happen next.

Managing Life on Overload

The advent of technology was supposed to make life easier for everyone. Quick access to information, the ability to complete tasks "on the fly," and increased communication were intended to free up time and allow people to focus on what matters to them. Unfortunately for most, it's done exactly the opposite. Increasing technology keeps many people connected 24/7, allowing for an overwhelming flood of information to come over the transom.

In many jobs, the need to check messages permeates family meals, vacations, and evening relaxation time. The ability to be online at all hours of the day or night checking for information and gaining access to new information to process is not soothing to most people; rather it increases the level of stress or worry.

In many cases, people struggle with time management. How can I get everything done in a given day? Children have places they must be; there are errands to run and tasks to complete; and on top of it all, the workplace continues to pile on more and more. The stress levels that the average person deals with seem to be increasing every day.

Stressed Much? You Bet!

The American Psychological Association found in a 2010 survey that "in general, Americans recognize that their stress levels remain high and exceed what they consider to be healthy.

Adults seem to understand the importance of healthy behaviors like managing their stress levels, eating right, getting enough sleep and exercise, but they report experiencing challenges practicing these healthy behaviors. They report being too busy as a primary barrier preventing them from better managing their stress, and a lack of motivation, energy, and time as the chief reasons for not being more physically active. Again in this study, lacking willpower was cited as a barrier to adopting healthy behaviors when lifestyle changes were recommended by a health care provider. Yet the majority believes willpower can be learned as well as improved, if they only had more energy and confidence."

Everyday Stress Builds

One of the problems with everyday stress is that it is insidious. You might not "feel" stressed, but all of a sudden you raise your voice in anger or begin to feel defeated and depressed. You notice that you are gritting your teeth or biting your nails. Everyday stress creeps in, and unbeknownst to you your negative self-talk fuels the stressful fires.

A car cuts you off on the freeway and you think, *What's wrong with people? The world is becoming such a rude and frightening place.* In the checkout line for ten items or less, someone gets in front of you with fifteen items. *See?* you say to yourself. *There are rude people everywhere. This world is really going to pot.* At home, where you want to enjoy the sanctuary of your abode, your child calls you some name not fit to repeat here. Your self-talk ceaselessly comments on these situations, and you mull over how awful everything has become and how terrible your life is.

This is how stress—and its partner in crime, negative self-talk—steals from you. They join forces and zap your energy, cloud your view, and give you a window on the world that is negative and self-defeating. Of course, you can explain it all: There really was a rude person on the freeway; someone did cut you in line; and your child really was disrespectful to you. The problem is, you then made a choice to let negative self-talk take over and pile on the trouble until you were unable to function in any positive way.

Uncovering What's Hidden

Like many of the things you will learn in this book, everyday stress is stealthy. It comes to you in situations you don't want. No one wants to be cut off on the freeway and put into danger, but rather than allow the situation to be what it is, a point in time, your mind likely grabs hold of it and turns it into a major negative event.

It's of the utmost importance with everyday stress to stay aware and alert to those things that trigger your negative self-talk. It takes commitment and energy to do this. You may resist because it is just easier to give in to the negativity. But you can, with strength of mind, change that. Moving from negative self-talk to positive self-talk is a choice. While you cannot control the events that happen to you, you can control your reaction to them.

Step Out of the Tornado

Some people walk through a tornado unscathed, and others are blown away by the winds. You can stand next to a raging emotional tornado but refuse to participate in it.

How? By becoming more conscious about the things you experience throughout your day that trigger negativity inside of you, and then by recognizing the negative responses that build upon themselves.

Stepping out of the tornado takes discipline. It requires being attentive to the things throughout the day that happen to you. For this exercise, it will be helpful to carry a small notebook with you at all times, or to use the note function on your smartphone or tablet. You want to keep a running list of things that occur to you so you can examine them with some distance.

Think of a time when you were going through something stressful in an everyday situation. For instance, perhaps you needed to be back home for your son's graduation, and you were due to catch a plane. You were caught in terrible traffic due to an accident on the freeway. You watched the clock tick, tick, tick while you sat immobile in your car and knew the plane would leave without you. Perhaps the plane did leave without you, and you raged or cried in the terminal knowing you would miss your son's smiling face as they handed him the diploma.

That was certainly a series of stressful and distressing events. But think about what happened next. Another flight left for your destination, and you eventually joined your son. You saw pictures of the graduation and were disappointed you weren't able to be there, but you did something to celebrate with your son, thereby enjoying his success. The stressful moment in the car watching that clock tick eventually faded from your memory. You talk about it in the past tense, as in, "Remember the time . . ."

The goal in stepping outside of the tornado is to call upon the post-experience while you are still in the experience. Even in the thick of difficulty, you realize "This too shall pass." In order to do this, you must call upon positive self-talk.

Resolve to keep a journal. For two weeks take notes of stressful situations throughout the day; this will help you to see patterns, triggers, and to get perspective on the things that seem stressful at the time, but later lose their power over you. As you embark on this process, resolve to capture everything you can. Don't overlook things that seem unimportant just because you are writing a journal! For example, you may be inclined to minimize an event because it seems silly to write it down. Be honest with yourself. There are no rights or wrongs—stress comes from many different directions for everyone. Capture everything to which your mind has a reaction or that you perceive as negative.

If you miss a day, continue noting occurrences until you have two weeks of data with which you can work. Be sure to capture not only the event but also your negative reaction to it. Next to the event, jot down a few words about the negativity you felt: "helpless," "overwhelmed," "angry."

Review your stressors. Once you have compiled the information, look through what you've written. Are there themes? Does it seem that some stressors occur more often than others? Is it a variety of stressors, some large and some small, or do you find that many small irritations happen throughout the day? Or conversely do you only get stressed by the seemingly big events?

Also, look at the descriptors you wrote next to the events. What themes do you see here? Do you most often respond with anger? Do you feel disillusioned a lot? Do you feel helpless and without resources to deal with stressors in your life?

It's critically important, before you can make positive self-talk work for you, that you have some awareness about the stressors and about your reactions. Don't skip these steps—take the time to explore your own situation in some detail.

Once you have more awareness of what stresses you and how you react, you can start to integrate positive self-talk into your day. Start the morning by using positive self-talk to frame your upcoming experiences. Use a mirror to talk to yourself for this initial exercise. Speak directly to yourself and put emphasis on the statements.

- "This is an ordinary day. There will be stressful things that happen to me. That's life. I have choices about how I can respond. I choose to keep my personal power today."
- "I can step outside of the tornado any time I want. I don't have to be dragged along by my own negative self-talk. As soon as I recognize it, I can release it. It's my choice."
- "Things will happen. I will react. Today I choose how I react, and I choose positive self-talk."
- "I welcome difficult situations because they almost always teach me something. They allow me to strengthen my attitude and practice my positive self-talk."
- "Life is for learning. I watch others. I watch situations. I learn something from everything that happens to me."
- "Holding on to my personal power is the most important thing to me. I stay focused on my positive approach throughout the day."

It's important that your self-talk statements are not phony to you. Throughout the day there will be things that trigger you. There will be events you probably don't want and would rather not deal with. There will be times you lapse into old behaviors. You are using these ideas to set your mind in a different direction, to react and respond differently to what will happen to you.

Now, create some positive self-talk options that you can call upon when stressors arise during the day. You might want to write these on 3" × 5" cards, or put them on notepaper you can carry around with you. Some people post these in their car, on their computer, or in their wallet. Keep them handy so you can refer to them when you need to.

Review the list and determine which of these suit your style and situation, or write a couple of your own using this same process.

- "Whatever life throws at me, I can deal with it. I am calm; I am confident; and I make my own choices."
- "Situations happen, but I don't need to fuel them with negative self-talk. I choose a different path."
- "Look at what's happening right now. It's a tornado, but I choose to step outside of it. The view is better from the outside looking in."
- "Tomorrow (or next month, next year, etc.) this situation probably won't even matter to me. I'm not going to give it my energy today."
- "Things happen. People are people. I don't need to make this situation worse with negative self-talk."

Then, importantly, when the stressful or negative event occurs, instead of giving in to negative self-talk, turn your attention to something that is positive for you. Some people carry a song with them that they like to sing. Some people carry pictures of children or animals that calm them. Some people take a walk, look outside the window, or do jumping jacks! Have something at the ready you can always do when the bothersome situation comes along.

How does this work in the real world? Imagine the situation with the car cutting you off on the freeway. Your immediate reaction is to make sure you are safe. Then, your chosen self-talk kicks in: "Things happen. People are people. I don't need to make this situation worse with negative self-talk." You begin to hum your calming song. Or you start to recall a fun vacation with your children. Perhaps you repeat your favorite verse from a poem. Your attention shifts from the situation at hand to something that calms you and is more peaceful. By now, the "rude" person has left your line of vision and is speeding off down the highway to cut off the next person—and possibly get a ticket. You, on the other hand, are driving along with a more peaceful attitude and demeanor.

Creating Time and Space for Recharging: Taking Care of Yourself

One of the ways that stress does damage is that in response to it many people stop taking care of themselves. They don't exercise or eat well. They lose sleep. They are too preoccupied or too busy to seek out friends or companions. They are in react mode as opposed to a deliberate planning mode.

Often when people need to take care of themselves most, they focus on it the least. Here is another place where turning to positive self-talk can help calm you and redirect your energies. The cycle goes like this: You feel stressed about events. You don't take care of yourself. You talk to yourself about how stupid you are that you don't take care of yourself. "I know I should get to the gym to alleviate my stress, but I am too wigged out to do so."

You know the choices you are making are not the right ones for you, but negative self-talk moves in again and reminds you that you need to behave the way you do, that you can't do anything better, and that this is all there is.

Starting Over

The beauty of recognizing how negative self-talk pulls you in and pulls you under is that at any point you can make a different decision about how you want to respond to your life. For example, if you know you "should" take better care of yourself but your self-talk doesn't let you, it's time to make a different decision.

First, ask yourself if there is something you could be doing differently, something that could help you more effectively deal with the stressors in your life. Do you need more sleep? Do you need to make better eating choices? Do you need to get more exercise? Set a goal for what you'd like to do. If you want to manage your stress by finding a new job or making more money, refer back to Chapter 7 for ways to use positive self-talk in making a life change. In this section, we'll deal with the need to take better care of yourself in order to be stronger in handling the general stressors in your life.

Determine what you need to do differently. Write here what you could do for yourself that might gain you more energy or be healthier as you manage stress.

_____

_____

Now write why you aren't doing this now. What's holding you back? What obstacles do you face? Be honest here and collect all of the reasons you are unable to make the choices you need to make. Be careful you aren't focusing on major life decisions in this section; those are addressed elsewhere in this book and involve a different set of exercises. For example, you might say you need to work out more often and get more exercise, but perhaps you are working three jobs. If this is the case, you need an overall life change. Refer to Chapter 7. In this section, though, you might write that you just can't stick to an exercise plan. You know you need one, but you never find anything that you enjoy enough to do over and over.

_____

_____

Identify the negative self-talk associated with your reasons for not being able to take the steps you know you need to take. These could be things like "I hate exercise" or "I can't afford to eat healthy food so I buy junk" or "I am just at that stage of life where I can't sleep very well. It happens to everyone."

Write the words you use and the things that come to mind if you were talking to another person and trying to convince her why you can't do what you know you should do.

_____

_____

In this next section, you will use your positive self-talk to change the behavior. First, set a goal for yourself that is reasonable, believable, and practical. For instance, you might set a goal: For the next five nights, I will go to bed fifteen minutes earlier each night until I am going to bed over an hour earlier than I have been." Or you might write, "I will choose carrots at the store when I shop this week instead of chips." Or, "I will take a walk each evening with my spouse for thirty minutes after dinner." Set a goal that you can reach and that moves you closer to your desired outcome. You are trying to make a life shift here, so you want to take this a step at a time. If you haven't been working out at all, setting a goal of working out six days a week for an hour is probably unrealistic. Focus on reasonable, believable, and practical.

_____

_____

Now, develop positive self-talk statements to help you with your efforts. These will be different depending on the goal you have chosen. If you have worked through other sections in this book, you will have some ideas about how to develop these. There are examples here for some common situations. You can use any of these, or write some of your own.

- "I want to make this shift in my life. It will help me manage my stress more easily."
- "Every day is a new day. Today I resolve to make the choices that are good for me."
- "My goal is reasonable. I can take steps each day to see that my goal becomes my reality."
- "I need all of the strength and resources I can get. I make the choices that give me more access to my personal resources."
- "Why in the world would I choose to do things that aren't good for me? I know what's right, and I choose in favor of me."

Once you have determined your goal, and have developed the positive self-talk that works for you, spend time each day for at least fifteen minutes sitting quietly and imaging a less stressed you. Picture yourself or think about yourself making the choices that are good for you. Imagine you are getting the sleep you need, eating the food you need, or taking walks each evening. Use all of your emotion and imagination to feel good about your accomplishments. Experience the good feelings that come from being calmer and more at ease, ready to deal with whatever comes your way.

As you sit and imagine, repeat your positive self-talk over and over again. Keep focused on what you *do* want, not what you *don't* want. Remember, to manage stress effectively you must have the tools to do so.

Taking Control of Your Time—and Your Life

There are few people in today's culture who wouldn't say they need more hours in the day. It never seems you have enough time to do all that you want to do, or need to do. Some people work two or three jobs and run from one to the other. Parents with children seem to have endless commitments: games and practices to attend, school events, play dates. In fact, most people in today's culture constantly have too many places to go and things to do. Life rolls on and on. Anxiety builds as the list of to-dos grows longer and longer.

Time is hard to manage when it offers you a fixed twenty-four hours a day, seven days a week. How can you control something that isn't flexible or malleable? Instead you must learn to manage yourself. Time management is about personal management.

Finish What You Start

For many people anxiety comes from the endless feeling that there are always things left to do. You might go to bed at night thinking about what has been left undone instead of what you have accomplished. The mind will grab on to what is open-ended and not addressed, and then negative self-talk will taunt you about what is still left to do. The truth is that you can never really finish everything that has to be done. As soon as the "to-do list" is completed, another one will pop up to take its place. But you can learn to manage your self-talk so that you take a different approach to the never-ending list of things to do.

Stop Watching the Clock

The first important step is to stop for a moment. Take your eyes off the clock and look at the long list of to-dos that you have accumulated. What's on that list? Are all of the things you need to do really important to you? Take a moment to prioritize things. What's most important and why? What's least important and why?

Reorder your to-do list so that instead of a random list of all you need to do, it's an organized and prioritized list of what must be done. You can use whatever criteria you want. You may decide that the easiest things should be highest priority because you can tackle them right away. Or, by contrast, you may give the harder things highest priority in order to get them over with. *What's important is to have a plan.* Have a methodology for going through your list that makes sense to you.

If you suffer from a feeling that time is escaping and you aren't conquering it, the exercise in this section should be used over and over again for many days. Remember, it takes at least twenty-one days to adopt a new habit. With time management it is best if you can do it for at least a month. Getting a handle on managing your personal and time-related issues is tricky. New things get added every day. Other people in your life may not "respect" your desire to change your approach and may continue to add items to your already overflowing plate. You have to be the one to take charge, and be consistent.

Step One

Make a list of the things that are outstanding that need to be managed. Start with a random list of everything that you currently have on your to-do sheet.

Step Two

Reorganize the list according to priority order. Number the items from 1 (most important) to 10 (least important). If you have more than ten items, put these on a separate list in priority order. For the purposes of this exercise, have no more than ten.

Step Three

Review your list of ten and see where you can break steps down into more discreet tasks. If, for example, you have to move your aging mother into a nursing home, and you have this as one "to-do," recognize instead that multiple steps are involved. There are probably ten or twelve things you need to do before you can accomplish this task. Take the to-do item and identify each piece in the process so you can see exactly what's involved. Sometimes dissecting the to-do and breaking it into smaller pieces actually changes the priority order. This is fine; change things around if you need to, but come up with a final list to work from.

Step Four

Now take each of the pieces on the to-do list and write an assumed time frame next to them. How long will each step take you? What's involved? Each to-do should have steps at this point and then time frames associated with them. You might end up with a page for each to-do; put the pages in priority order with the most important one on top. You may want to have a file folder for each of the to-dos, but be sure to code them by priority order, whatever method you are using.

Step Five

Now review to see whether there is anything you can delegate to someone else. Are there pieces that other people could do for you? What creative ways could you use to accomplish some of the things on the list?

Step Six

Next, move the steps for the first three priority to-dos, along with their associated time frames, onto a calendar. When will you do these things? What day? What time? Who else might you engage? Write it down. Review this each night or first thing in the morning so you have the plan for the day.

Step Seven

Now bring your positive affirmations into the process. Each day when you are reviewing your to-do list or writing your steps down in your calendar, you want to be aware of any negative self-talk that tells you it is "just too much to do." Use some of the positive self-talk listed here over and over again. Remember to do this for at least a month.

- "Time is a man-made construct. I am in charge of my time; it is not in charge of me."
- "I can say 'no' the next time someone asks me to take something on if I don't feel I can do it. My life belongs to me."
- "Taking steps one at a time allows me to work through my to-do list and get something done every single day."
- "I have taken the time to organize, prioritize, and break steps down. I know what's important and what I need to focus on."
- "I refuse to allow myself to be drawn into anxiety about what I need to do. I stand outside the anxious state, being watchful and making my plans."
- "I can do what I need to do. I focus on my priorities."
- "Worrying about what I need to do and experiencing anxiety makes me less effective. I am effective and productive."
- "I am clear about what I need to do, and I do it."
- "I feel good about what I accomplish each day. I am in charge of my life."

Practicing good self-management of time can benefit you in many ways. You will become more efficient at work, more productive at home, as well as less stressed about what you need to do.

Releasing Stressors

This chapter has covered a number of different aspects related to stress. You may have previously thought stress was just a natural and common response to life's problems, but now you have seen that stress and anxiety visit in a variety of different ways. If stress is running your life, review this chapter to decide which aspects you want to begin to practice to become calmer and more at peace. You are not as effective when you are living life on stressful overload. Replacing negative self-talk with more positive approaches is available to you in many different situations.

CHAPTER 9

The Art of Self-Reflection: Challenging Your Self-Talk

Before reading this book, you probably believed that your self-talk was you. You didn't realize that it's a separate thing whispering in your ear and calling the shots—most of which have led you to anxiety and unhappiness. If you are like many people, you have probably been listening to it for most of your life and taking whatever negative path it presented to you.

Listening to negative self-talk and acting on its "wisdom" seemed natural. You probably became so used to its voice that you didn't realize that it was talking to you and making everything you deal with more difficult than it needed to be. While negative self-talk did its dirty work, your anxiety rose. Any opportunity you had for a calmer you went out the window along with your objectivity.

This is why negative self-talk is so insidious. It feels like a part of you. It visits; you welcome it and recognize it; and then it stays. But now, as a result of going through the exercises in this book and thinking about them, you know how much it is stealing from you and how many possibilities have passed you by because you have been engaged in a dialogue with something that doesn't have your best interests at heart. You have taken the first most important step to remove negative self-talk from your life. You are making a commitment to uninvite it and to welcome new ideas and new possibilities that calm your mind and give you back your natural energy.

To Lose It, You Have to Know It

In order to uninvite negative self-talk, as you have learned throughout this book, you have to become aware of how it visits you and refuse to let it move in and take hold of you. Self-reflection is important, and you have to first admit to yourself that negative self-talk has been stealing your calm and derailing your hopes and dreams. Negative self-talk does nothing but steal from you. It isn't your friend. It isn't even telling you the truth—it's telling you sad and worrisome stories that are made up. Negative self-talk feeds on anxiety, stress, and upset. It takes hold and increases your pain. It's time to take your life back and tell yourself a different story.

Recognizing the Visitor

The more aware you become of how and when negative self-talk visits you, the more choices you will have to deal with it when it does. In Chapter 2 you completed an assessment to understand where some of your anxiety comes from. Review this list now. You were asked to circle six things that are particular causes of anxiety for you. In addition, you've likely read through other sections of this book and found other places your negative self-talk has taken over.

Take a minute now to capture the things you have learned about your own anxiety.

1. Anxiety most often visits me when: _____

   _____

2. Situations that make me especially anxious include:

   _____

   _____

3. I have realized I use negative self-talk in the following areas: _____

   _____

If you still feel vague, or as if anxiety visits you all throughout the day in many different situations, as it does for many people, keep a journal. Identify the things that happen to you throughout the day that kick your negative self-talk into action. Note the event, or the thought, and then the words that you use to tell yourself there is, or could be, a problem. The more you become aware of when and how negative self-talk visits you, the more choices you have for offering it the invitation to leave. Dedicate yourself to this. Choose in favor of yourself and your life and commit to awareness.

Your Personal Toolkit

Not everything works for every person. This chapter will offer a variety of tried-and-true techniques you can use to both stop negative self-talk in its tracks and put you on a more successful path to positive outcomes you desire. This chapter provides choices for your personal toolkit. The more tools you have to deal with life's ups and downs, the more power you will have in the midst of whatever happens to you.

Tool 1: The Power of Self-Hypnosis

Many people don't trust hypnosis. The possibility that another person could take hold of your mind and give you ideas may seem frightening. A good hypnotist helps you to see where your mind is hampering you and giving you ideas that aren't in your best interest. She offers hypnotic suggestions for a better life. Self-hypnosis is a tool you can bring to bear at any time. It can be used anywhere to calm you, center you, and get you back on track with your positive self-talk.

Practice Really Does Make Perfect

Like everything else you have learned in this book, practicing will make you more effective. You have "practiced," unknowingly, using negative self-talk. It will take practice to learn new, healthy behaviors.

To employ self-hypnosis and use it effectively, take the following steps:

1. Develop a positive, calming "trigger." You can do this by sitting in a quiet place to relax. It should be somewhere you will not be interrupted and that is relaxing and comfortable for you. Have your back supported, your feet flat on the floor, and your hands resting loosely in your lap. Close your eyes.

2. Take three deep breaths. Breathe in deeply through your nose. Imagine there is a deflated balloon in your stomach and you are filling it with your breath. See the balloon fill as you breathe deeply in. Breathe out through your mouth and imagine the balloon deflating as you do. It's important that your breathing is centered on your stomach area and not your chest. Breathing through the stomach allows you to take deep, cleansing breaths.

3. Sit quietly with your eyes closed and focus on your breathing. Allow your breathing to continue in a calm and soothing fashion. Do your best to empty your mind of thoughts and feelings. When thoughts come in, gently push them away. Imagine there is a janitor with a broom

who gently pushes out any thought or feeling that tries to enter. Your goal is to leave your mind open and receptive to positive ideas.

4. When you are ready, and your mind is open, focus on something that is soothing to you. For some people it is hearing the waves at the beach. For others it is walking through a forest on a crisp morning listening to birds and the crunch of the leaves. Others may imagine taking a warm bath or sitting by a fire. Allow your mind to hold the image of a place where you feel at peace. Make it a place where you are rested, relaxed, and calm. Continue to focus on this until you feel your body letting go. Let your muscles relax. Let your shoulders droop and release any tension. Move your head and neck if need be to release tension that gathers here. Allow your body, along with your mind, to simply slip into a calm, beautiful, and serene imagined place.

5. When you feel your body releasing and you can really embrace the feeling of being calm and centered, it's time to establish your personal trigger. Put the first three fingers of your hand (your thumb, your forefinger, and your middle finger) together and form a touchpoint. Allow these fingers to touch and in your mind associate the touching with your relaxed and calm state. In your mind, say, "Every time I touch these three fingers together, I become calm and relaxed." Say this over and over gently to yourself. Don't force it, but allow

the sensation to permeate. Be aware as you say this of how calm and relaxed you feel. If you want a different trigger, you can touch your toes together as you sit there. Associate your toes gently touching with your relaxed state. Again, repeat to yourself, "Every time I touch my toes, anywhere I am, I immediately feel relaxed and calm." It's important to create an association so that anywhere, at any time, you can call upon the trigger to send a message to your body to calm.

Do this exercise at least twice a day for five to seven minutes. Once you master the process, you can do this anywhere. You might put your seat back in your car and practice this in a parking lot. (Be sure to lock your doors before you do so in order to stay safe.) You can do this before you go to bed at night, but be sure to sit upright so that you don't fall asleep in the process.

Your trigger will be with you at all times. Every time you feel anxiety rising, or a negative response about to occur, you can engage your trigger and send a message to your body to become calm and more centered in that moment.

Tool 2: Become a Friend to Yourself

One of the ways that negative self-talk steals from you is that it visits you as a friend. It pretends it can fix something for you by telling you stories about what's going to happen next, and how you need to respond.

This tool helps you really become your own best friend. It involves the art of stepping outside of your mind as it is talking to you and viewing what's happening to you. What does this mean? It means developing the ability to be more objective and watchful about what you do, what you think, and how you approach things. This process allows you to be more objective and more curious about what you think and why you think it. It is not about judging or criticizing but rather about learning and being interested in the "why?"

1. Resolve that you want to learn more about what you think, how negative self-talk creeps in, and how it steals from you. Instead of diminishing the impact it has on you, you choose instead to learn about it. Think of this as a learning process—the intention is to take a serious interest in what's happening. As well, it's important to use this process to stay aware of where and how negative self-talk visits you. You can't become detached and aware if you don't even know what's happening!

2. Adopt an air of curiosity and become a detective. Rather than using more negative self-talk ("See, there I go! I am always beating up on myself! Didn't I learn anything from reading this book?"), you will now become more curious, more interested in what is happening. Instead of reacting to it, you want to explore and learn from it. So, for example, you might say to yourself the next time you are perusing social media and see a friend is taking a trip,

"Hmmm. That's so interesting. I am reading someone's posts about a cruise she's taking and now my negative self-talk is coming to life about how I will never be able to take a vacation again. Why do I let it talk to me and make me feel worse? It's interesting how just reading this one post set my negativity into motion. I need to watch out for that the next time I read Facebook posts. It's fascinating to see how my mind took hold and then used that post against me. I will be much more aware next time." You are not criticizing or trying to fix the problem. You are simply acknowledging it's there. You are recognizing a relationship between an event and your ensuing negative self-talk. By recognizing it, the next time you will be more aware of the connection.

3. Remember that anytime, anywhere, you have the ability to remove yourself from an emotional reaction and react with objectivity and interest. You always have the choice to say "Hmmmm. Isn't that interesting?" instead of responding in a negative, emotional fashion. It's the emotional pull that causes the anxiety and smashes the calm. Step outside to view it, and don't give in to it next time.

If you want, you can also use this tool to tell yourself a different story. One of the nice things about being an objective outsider looking at your own life and thoughts is that it gives you the chance to rewrite the script! Once you recognize the unfolding of negativity and make a choice not to judge it, you can choose a different story ending. For example, you could say, "Yes, my friend is going on a cruise. Good for her and her family. It doesn't impact my life at all. In fact, I realize I have a distaste for cruising! I think I will turn my attention to something else right now." And then you do. You turn your attention to something you like, or that engages you. Perhaps you start to put one of your plans into place, or maybe you use your positive self-talk to work toward a goal. Whatever it is, you deliberately turn away from the negativity and take yourself mentally down another path.

Tool 3: Telling Yourself a Different Story

The amazing thing about self-talk is that you probably don't realize how often you are engaged in storytelling. Storytelling has been around for thousands of years. All of the great spiritual teachers used it, and effective marketers use it today to "sell" their wares. Why is it so powerful? Because people love stories. They understand stories. They can relate to stories. Stories draw people in and give them something to hold on to.

The problem with the stories you have been telling yourself with your negative self-talk is that they don't have a happy ending! We want to turn them around and write positive, happy endings instead.

The Power of Storytelling

According to AdWeek.com, "There is a growing body of research that points to the power of narrative not just as a way to engage people, but as the only way to change deeply entrenched views." If you like stories, you might be able to add storytelling to your toolkit as a way to change your own deeply entrenched views about the world and its impact on you.

Changing your stories involves recognizing the ones you are telling yourself now. Like the rest of the exercises in this book, the first step is awareness. You have to realize where the stories come in and start to talk to you and what they say. Stories are compelling and gripping. Right now the stories you tell yourself are not ones that calm you, or you would not be reading through this book.

To use this tool, you must become aware of the way that negative self-talk looks at a situation, then tells you about it, and then tells you the way the story is going to end.

Let's say, as an example, that you really want to get married. You had a blind date this week that didn't turn out well. Your negative self-talk on the way home from the date told you, "What a loser. I am a magnet for idiots. I will never find someone."

Then the story starts to evolve out of the negative self-talk. You might tell yourself that you never deserve to be married. That your childhood tainted you forever. You might talk about your future as an "old maid," never having children or learning what it's like to be romanced and seduced. You might go on and on and on about your friends and their lives and compare yourself. Before you know it, you have written your life story relative to this issue. You know how the story ends, and you "give up" because there isn't any point in continuing.

1. To break the cycle and tell yourself more engaging and behavior-changing stories, first become aware of how the negative reaction turns into a story about the way your life will go. Write in your journal (if you haven't started one by this time, start it now) about situations that upset you or bother you. Identify your negative self-talk associated with them. Review what you have written and see if you can connect or understand how the "story" goes from simply a negative reaction to a fait accompli.

2. Next, look at the situation you have written in your journal. Make up another story about how it could develop. You can have fun with this. Perhaps tell a story about a woman who was on a bus one day and found the love of her life. She wasn't looking for it, but all of a sudden there he was! You can make your story fun, and you can make it in the third person if it doesn't feel right to talk about yourself. The important thing is to create the new story. Keep embellishing it. You can make it dramatic and complex or basic and simple. It doesn't matter—it's your story! You are writing the plot line,

the characters, and the ending. Make your endings happy ones.

It may seem silly, but this actually orients your mind to more positive things. You might find yourself smiling or just feeling happy when you engage in the storytelling process. It often brings a sense of hope and optimism. It is why, as children, many enjoy fairy tales and happy endings. We want the good guys to win, and the bad guys to be punished—in most cases. Make sure that you, as the good guy or gal with the starring role, come out a winner in all of your stories.

Tool 4: Using the STOP! Technique

Sometimes it's necessary to interrupt the flow of negative thoughts and feelings in your mind by doing something a bit dramatic. The STOP! approach involves first noticing the negative thoughts are there and then choosing to stop them in their tracks.

1. When a negative thought or feeling comes upon you, and you notice it because it drains your energy and you feel either angry, depressed, or defeated, you must first realize the negativity is there.
2. Imagine a red stop sign at the end of a street leading to an intersection. Say out loud to yourself, "STOP!" Interrupt the flow. Tell your mind to stop in its tracks. Stop the rolling thoughts as you would stop the rolling car before

it enters the intersection. Say to yourself, "I choose to STOP!" And then do. Just stop. Don't wonder. Don't ruminate. Don't question. Just stop.

3. It can be helpful to have a positive thought to replace the negative one. If you have a mantra that you like or a prayer, meditation, or song that makes you feel good, have this ready. Once you stop the negative flow, turn to the positive and uplifting thoughts. You may call upon one of the positive self-talk sentences you have learned throughout this book. You may just call upon a one- or two-line song that has always made you feel good. Whatever you have in your toolkit, bring it out now and focus on it. The important key is to stop the ruminating, and then replace it with something more positive and more resourceful.

4. Do this as many times as you need to until the negative self-talk has left. Continue to replace the negativity with something positive. STOP the negativity right in its tracks before it can add more fuel to your worry or anxiety. You can stop it—choose to do so.

Tool 5: Finding a Partner

The insidious thing about negative self-talk is that many people don't want to admit to others that they engage in it and that it is hurting them. It just seems natural to talk to yourself about what you see, what you think about it, and how it might impact you. All the while your mind is unsettled and anxiety is rising. Having a buddy, or a partner, can be very useful because it means you can bring negative self-talk to the surface and question it. When you begin to talk to others, you will find that many people suffer the consequences of negative self-talk in a variety of ways.

1. If possible, identify someone in your life who seems ill at ease. Perhaps the person worries too much, or tells you about his concerns. He might talk about situations in a negative light. This person may need your help, and in turn you could benefit from his assistance. Approach him and let him know you are reading this book and have become committed to working with your negative self-talk and turning it into something more positive and healthy. Ask him if he'd be willing to be a "buddy" with you. Pick someone that you can trust and with whom you would be comfortable sharing your thoughts and feelings in some detail.

2. First, establish some parameters. Will you check in each day? Will you check in when you feel overwhelmed by the negative self-talk? Will you check in via e-mail or via phone? How will you work together to help one another? Next, you want to establish what you will talk about. Do you want to each identify one to three incidents during a time period where you resorted to negative self-talk and it was not beneficial? Do you want to practice turning

negative self-talk into positive self-talk together? Do you want to explore options with one another about what you could have said, or done? Last, have a follow-up plan. It's not enough to just identify what's happening—you have to have agreement with one another about what you will do differently. You want to observe the places where you get into trouble but also celebrate the progress you are making.

3. Use the following template for working with your partner to take hold of your anxiety and calm your anxious mind with more positive self-talk.

- Name of my partner: _____
- When we will connect: _____
- How we will connect: _____
- Our objective together:_____
- Ground rules for our working together: _____

  _____

- Our follow-up plans each time we speak: _____

  _____

The more you can discuss up front the manner in which you will interact together, the better outcome you will have. You will find you benefit from having another person who is open to learning more and willing to talk about his experiences.

Tool 6: Handy Affirmations

There are a number of different general affirmations you can use at any time and put into your personal toolkit. Refer back to the assessment you completed in Chapter 2. You were asked to identify areas that are particularly unsettling to you and that create anxiety. You may have identified things that are harder to pin down, such as a general lack of self-worth or guilt over things you have done in the past. These may not be tied to a specific catalyst or event. They may come upon you at any point in time and cause your mind to get anxious and upset.

As you have learned, the way negative self-talk works is that it sneaks in unannounced. You may be going about your day thinking you are reasonably content and happy, and all of a sudden an agitation starts within. Probably what has happened is that negative self-talk has picked up on one of the things that makes you anxious—say, thinking about past trouble you have been in—and it begins to talk to you about what a jerk you were, how you can never make up for the trouble you caused, and what a terrible person you turned out to be!

Because of this dynamic, you need some general affirmations to carry around with you that you can call upon at any time. Unlike the other positive self-talk you have learned about, which is connected to specific situations or desires, these are more general affirmations to be used in any circumstance. Like the other tools in your toolkit, you hold on to these and bring them out when you need them.

Positive Affirmations for All Occasions

- "Every day in every way, I am getting better and better" (attributed to Émile Coué).
- "Life *is* fundamentally good. It is only my attitude that needs to change for the better."
- "I move toward happiness and contentment every day."
- "I can choose to be calm any time by taking three deep breaths."
- "Worry is wasted energy that I might need if trouble ever does come my way. I save my energy to deal with things as they come and when I need to."
- "I choose happiness."
- "I can uninvite negative thoughts and feelings anytime I choose. I picture myself letting them go."
- "I think positive thoughts. I feel positive feelings. I am a positive person."

- "Life is filled with obstacles, but so what? People have been overcoming obstacles since the beginning of time. So can I."
- "I am in charge of my thoughts and my feelings."
- "Feeling negative is a waste of time. I am only given so many days on this earth, and I want to make the most of the ones I am given."
- "I deliberately turn my attention to a positive step I can take."
- "I can always choose to do just one thing differently."
- "I hold the power to choose in favor of myself. I choose calm. I choose contentment. I choose peace."
- "I am capable. I make good decisions. I only need to change my mindset and my self-talk, and my situation can change."
- "I make my mind a blank. Instead of worrying, stressing, or giving in to anxiety, I choose to allow my mind to be a blank canvas. What's painted on the canvas next will be good for me. I am drawn to positive outcomes."

Packing Your Toolkit

Review the options available to you in this chapter. It can be helpful to test out more than one and see what works best for you. And on some days, you may need to call upon a number of different tools. You may find that one tool works great in one situation, and another works well for something else. Use them where they're appropriate. (Don't close your eyes or use self-hypnosis when you are driving, for example. Don't tell your stories out loud to people who don't know what you are doing.) Be sure you check time and place and call upon the right tool at the right time.

The good news is that you can use all of these tools in different situations. Remember that you are powerful and you have ways to respond to those situations that have caused you anxiety in the past. You can calm your own anxious mind by taking the right steps. You are making a decision to start taking those steps right now.

Good luck on your journey!

Index

About the Author

Beverly D. Flaxington, the Human Behavior Coach, is a two-time bestselling and Gold-award winning author. She is a corporate consultant and trainer, an executive coach, a successful entrepreneur, a Hypnotherapist and Hypnosis Trainer, a college professor, a motivational public speaker, and a Certified Behavioral and Values Analyst. Bev's work has been featured in hundreds of media outlets including the *Wall Street Journal*, MSNBC.com, *Reader's Digest*, *USA Today*, and many others.

She is a proven expert in human behavior and change management, sales, marketing, stress management, hypnosis, time management, life and career change, teambuilding, communication, and business building. Bev is also devoted to animal rescue and currently has seven pets of her own in addition to multiple fosters. She lives in Massachusetts with her husband and three children.